Signs of Taste

D1622270

Signs of Taste

A Gastrological Guide and Recipe Book

Steven Mark Weiss

Breitenbush Books
Portland, Oregon

Copyright © 1988 by Steven Mark Weiss
All Rights Reserved.

This book, or any part thereof, may not be reproduced by any means, written or mechanical, or be programmed into any electronic retrieval or information storage system without permission in writing from the publisher, except where short passages are used solely for the purpose of review in periodicals, television, or radio.

First edition: 2 3 4 5 6 7 8 9

Library of Congress Cataloging in Publication Data

Weiss, Steven M.
    Signs of taste: a gastrological guide and recipe book / Steven Mark Weiss. —
1st ed.
        p. cm.
    Includes index.
    ISBN 0-932576-59-1 (pbk.)
    1. Cookery 2. Astrology I. Title.
TX652.W395 1988
641.5—dc19   88-11730
                                                                                    CIP

Breitenbush Books are published by Breitenbush Publications, PO Box 02137, Portland, Oregon 97202.
Patrick Ames, Editor-in-Chief.
Text design by Susan Applegate of Publishers Book Works, Inc.
Cover design by Susan Gustavson
Cover photography by Richard Embery

Distributed by Taylor Publishing Company,
1550 W. Mockingbird Lane, Dallas, Texas 75235
Manufactured in the U.S.A.

For the
teachers and students
of astrology, cooking and writing
with the hope that their fields may flourish
in the twenty-first century

Acknowledgments

A large portion of thanks to everyone who took the time to answer the Survival Cuisine or Breakfast Epiphanies questionnaires. Second helpings for the recipes.

Thanks to Jim Anderson, Lisa Ekus and their staffs for being so damn smart.

Thanks to all the family, friends and professional associates who have managed some curiosity, enthusiasm and occasional acceptance of this weird, weird stuff.

And to Suzanne Rosenberg Weiss, who has taught me everything I will ever need to know about ice cream, thanks for always leaving a light on in the refrigerator.

The author and publisher gratefully acknowledge permission to use copyright material as follows:

Hans Christian Anderson, from "The Travelling Companion," in *Fairy Tales of Hans Christian Anderson*, Orion Press 1958 (Crown Publishers); James Beard, from "A Word of Advice," in *The Fireside Cookbook*, Simon & Schuster 1949; M.F.K. Fisher, from "The Measure of My Powers," in *The Art of Eating*, Macmillan Vintage Books 1976, copyright 1937, 1941, 1942, 1943, 1948, 1949, renewed 1971, 1976, 1977 by M.F.K. Fisher; Richard Ben Cramer, from "What Do You Think of Ted Williams Now?", in *Esquire*, June 1986, copyright Stirling Lord Literistic, Inc.; Truman Capote, from "Master Misery," in *A Capote Reader*, Random House, Inc. 1987; Woody Allen, dialogue from the movie *Sleeper*, MGM/UA Communications Co. and Mr. Allen; Neil Diamond, from "Porcupine Pie," on *Hot August Nights*, MCA Records, copyright 1972 Prophet Music; Adelle Davis, from *Let's Cook It Right*, copyright 1947, 1962 by Harcourt Brace Jovanovich, Inc., renewed 1975 by Frank Vernon Sieglinger. Reprinted by permission of the publisher.

Contents

Introduction

A few years back I was attending a national conference on gastronomy and, at a luncheon, suddenly found myself sitting next to Julia Child.

I had always wanted to meet this great culinary star, and had in fact spent a fair amount of the three-day conference stalking the French Chef. There had been plenty of opportunities when I could have walked right up to her and said hello, but I didn't want to seem like just a gastronomic groupie. I wanted our meeting to be memorable.

Julia introduced the speaker at the conference's final meal function and, stepping away from the podium, she scanned the crowded dining room for a place to sit. As fate would have it, the only available seat close by was immediately on my right. She took it.

I sat there in a state of frozen dumb, pretending to listen to the speaker. But all my brain kept repeating was "Wow, it's really Julia Child." I was by now definitely feeling silly, but I was frozen and the minutes rushed by.

The speaker finished and I was resigned to losing my opportunity. By this time I was willing to settle for a simple return to mobility. But instead of leaving the table, as I'd anticipated, Julia turned towards me.

"Lunch was quite good, don't you think?"

She spoke to me. Julia Child asked me a question.

Whatever was the answer?

Lunch had in fact been quite good, one of the best meals of the conference. Prepared by a renowned young California chef, the effort was a masterful display of the light and natural "spa cuisine" style. The food was most successful in its unexpectedly exciting mélange of spicy flavors, which even managed to trump the *de rigeur* floral fantasia of the plate arrangements.

"Yes it was," was all I could manage, some thirty seconds after the question had been asked.

Julia smiled politely and turned away from me towards the individual on her right. At last I conceded to myself that if any significant contact were going to be made, it would have to be via the slightly mad gambit from which there would be no return.

"Julia," I suddenly croaked, making so bold as to touch her arm.

She turned towards me again.

"I have a question," I managed to continue, "which I bet no one has ever asked you at one of these food conferences."

"Oh?" she said intrigued, tilting her head slightly, eyebrows cautiously bidding me to proceed.

She waited patiently as I began to rummage through the briefcase propped against my chair. Finding my quarry I brandished it briefly before slapping it down on the table. It was a copy of Julia Child's natal horoscope.

"Were you really born at 11:30 p.m. in Pasadena?" I asked, trying to make it sound like the world's most reasonable question.

She was definitely startled. I knew this because her body involuntarily jerked backwards, slightly upsetting her chair. Fearing I'd made a huge mistake, I simply sat grinning at her to express a sort of harmless intent. And after a few long moments, she began edging back towards the table.

She gazed at the piece of paper before her, at the carefully drawn twelve-slice pie with its numbered cookie-cutter garnishes. Her eyes travelled to her name and date of birth at the top of the paper. She then uttered the phrase, with that wonderful voice that is certainly the most recognizable in the food universe, from which I date the true involvement of the professional food community in gastrology:

"What does this mean?"

● ● ●

A few months before meeting Julia, I had given a talk on menu trends at the Chicago-based convention of the National Restaurant Association.

It was 1984, and at that particular time in American culinary history it appeared, if one was to believe the food journals, that Americans were becoming incredibly devoted to such menu items as cheese made from the milk of goats, itty-bitty vegetables arranged on a plate to look like temple mosaics, and a variety of esoteric lettuces that at one point everyone had stopped eating because of bitterness but now wanted to eat for exactly that same reason. There was truly a kind of grim wackiness to the emergent menu trends of 1984, as affluent and inflationary times begged for novelty but an image-conscious population stipulated nutritional restraint and gourmet aesthetics.

Still, there was no way I was going to appear before a diverse group of American restaurant operators and tell them that the American public's major menu concern had become vegetable chic. The professionals expected to hear about sandwiches and fried foods and melted cheese appetizers and alcoholic beverages—the menu items that kept and continue to keep most of them in business. For if that part of the business was in serious trouble, there would be no zucchini small enough to reverse the damage.

What occurred to me while preparing my talk was to approach several dozen members of the professional food community—leading food editors, successful restaurateurs, well-known chefs, important food service marketing executives, i.e., the purveyors of the grim wackiness—for the purpose of inquiring as to their personal dietary practices. Were *they* diligently grazing on bitter forage? Or were they actually going home and calling out for pizzas like the rest of us?

"What ten foods and/or beverages," was the lead-off inquiry on a four-page questionnaire that I entitled *Survival Cuisine*, "would you want to have with you if you were stranded on a deserted island?"

Some of the things mentioned most often: bread, cheese, chicken, hamburgers, wine, ice cream, chocolate. Some of the things mentioned hardly at all: bitter lettuce, goat cheese, itty-bitty vegetables. The consensus wasn't all that surprising.

To be truthful, though, there were a lot of idiosyncratic preferences revealed on the personal lists. Some of the "experts" could not bear the thought of abandoning Belon oysters or Calamata olives, while still others felt equally strongly about Jell-O and Velveeta cheese-product. In my presentation to the National Restaurant Association, I gave a perfunctory nod to these indices of the breadth in human tastes, without really attempting to emphasize their major significance amidst my "everyman" conclusions.

Howsoever, my remarks did not go unnoticed. In Chicago, both the *Tribune* and the *Sun-Times* published extensive coverage of my survey results and, in the highest form of recognition that can be granted someone with a string of strange statistics, my study was summarized in a front page box in *USA Today*. These papers, and those that carried the story from the wire services, seemed to enjoy announcing the punctured pretensions of the experts.

Sensing that I was on to something I continued to administer the questionnaire, no longer confining myself to professionally-ranked foodies but soliciting the input of family, friends and casual acquaintances as well. The general consensus continued in a moderate and expected vein, but the idiosyncrasies also multiplied. After I'd completed a few hundred of these interviews, however, I began to notice that there was even a tendency towards thematic consistency in the idiosyncrasies.

I'm certainly glad that I asked everyone their astrological sign.

• • •

It does not matter if you believe in astrology. It can still be useful and it can still be fun. Perhaps the very best thing about it is that it attempts to explain and thereby encourage the acceptance of things that tend to defy explanation or easy acceptance.

Why do some people eat at McDonald's a lot?

Why do some people like anchovies on their pizza?

Why do some people need *kung pao* shrimp in order to survive?

Nobody can really say why. But these things are true. And there is just something that's almost convincing and definitely entertaining in using astrology to explore such matters.

Let me confess a real desire to heavy-up here. I've written several drafts of this introduction in which I've become very serious at this point, going into urgent philosophical and historical defenses and explications of the tradition of gastrology. But let's face it, you'd have turned to the chapter on your own sun sign long before you got through that.

If I may be allowed one slight indulgence, though, my editor and I both particularly like the following:

Through the many centuries of human evolution, mankind's artists, magicians, sages, and saints have linked manna with heavenly mystery. Ambrosia for the sky travellers of Olympus. Communion with the Heavenly Host. Alice growing tall.

Allow me to also reiterate that "science" has not been entirely plucked and parboiled in the preparation of this manuscript. The information presented here was obtained through hundreds of serious and lengthy personal interviews and questionnaire responses. The observations are statistically valid, at least within this sample group, and qualities not portrayed by a majority of the respondents of each astrological sign have not been attributed to them.

The rest *is* voodoo eat-onomics.

• • •

I did not do a great job of reading Julia's chart. I was nervous and the situation was more than a little awkward. Perhaps, I couldn't help thinking, she was only humoring me until hotel security could arrive.

I was dying to tell her of the rare correspondences between our two horoscopes: my Saturn exactly conjunct her Mercury; her Mars exactly conjunct my mid-heaven; and especially her Sun exactly conjunct my Moon in exact opposition to my Sun. It would have sounded immodest. Hell, it would have sounded insane.

There was no turning back, though, and once again the second hand was sweeping through the silence. With her Jupiter (a planet of insight and worldly good fortune) in Sagittarius (the sign ruled by Jupiter) conjunct her seventh house cusp (partnerships), I decided I could analytically move towards those grounds without offending. So I told her that the people she chose to become closely involved with would always broaden her understanding and bring good fortune to her.

Her eyelids fluttered and she mumbled acknowledgment. She again looked intently at her chart and I once more fell to silence. Maybe thirty seconds passed.

"Can I have this?," she suddenly asked.

"Sure," I responded cheerily. "Can I sign it?"

"Sure," said Julia.

I tore the paper a little as I pressed down on the linen table cloth. Actually, my signature ended up looking as if I'd held the pen between my teeth. Probably enhance its value to a gastrological historian.

Julia smiled, thanking me as she rose. I rose too, but as soon as her back was turned I looked at my watch.

It was 1:12 p.m. Pacific standard time January 25, 1985, in Santa Barbara, California.

A Note on Recipes

This book is called a recipe book for the specific purpose of distinguishing it from a cookbook. Cookbooks emphasize technical accuracy and consistency. A recipe book is simply a collection of ideas.

The recipes in this book are presented here for the very reason that they graphically reflect the culinary styles, abilities and interests of the various contributors. They are most useful here insofar as they reflect personality, so there has been no effort made to remove some most-entertaining and instructive culinary asides, or to get by without including two recipes for cheese cake or Chicken Divan.

Note: In the recipes, T. is used for tablespoon, t. for teaspoon. All oven temperatures are in Fahrenheit.

Aries

March 21 to April 19

Then all the people shouted "Hurrah!" The band played music in the street, the bells rang and the cake-women took the black crepe off the sugar sticks. There was universal joy. Three oxen, stuffed with ducks and chickens, were roasted whole in the market place, where everyone might help himself to a slice. The fountains spouted forth the most delicious wine, and whoever bought a penny loaf at the baker's got six large buns, full of raisins, as a present.

In the evening the whole town was lighted up. The soldiers fired off cannons, and the boys let off crackers. There was eating and drinking, dancing and jumping everywhere.

Hans Christian Andersen (Aries), fabler
from "The Travelling Companion"

We ran around that supermarket at 2 a.m., seeing which one of us could assemble the best meal for five people with seven dollars' worth of ingredients. We had five minutes and the store manager announced it over the microphone.

Laurie Vacha (Aries), professional chef

Aries' blessing and curse is an abundance of energy. Active, radiant, rampant, full-speed-ahead energy. The kind of energy that a bighorn packs into a headlong assault, or a roaring fire throws into the darkness.

Insatiable doers, Aries prefer action above all else, including accuracy, and sometimes even including attainment. They have such indomitable spirits that they often seem to court certain resistance and failure. As long as the pot continues to boil....

An Aries may be encountered in any activity which emphasizes the "I" in independence, intrepidness, idealism, intensity and immediate gratification. Come hell or high water, Aries want to find it, live it, be it, exploit it now. They crave exploration, enterprise and life in the fast lane.

So what are they like when they're hungry?

Well, first, an Aries can always use a cold soft drink or a glass of iced tea. People of continuous waking activity, they deeply require the pauses that refresh—although they will likely drink Coke rather than Pepsi because Coke was first. Whatever the specific beverage, an Aries will have a great fondness for ice.

In fact, anything that melts—butter, ice cream, frozen yogurt—is likely to be an Aries favorite. They love the principle of heat overcoming cold, of energy overcoming inertia (Aries regard the unmelted ice cream in a Baked Alaska with something close to religious awe). In cooking they like high heat, the sort that rattles the pots and chars the flesh.

Generally, Aries are marked by bold and experimental tastes, and they have good instincts about nutrition. Under all circumstances Aries are disposed towards trying the new, and they always seem to be among the first to be in on such trends as Thai cuisine, tapas bars and fruit wedges stuffed into beer bottles. By the same token, they will abandon trends that have become too widespread, as they have a deep-seated fear of being mistaken for followers.

In nutritional matters, Aries are occasional faddists (provided they can be among the first to employ the new wonder-regimen), but they are hardly ever fanatical about dietary lore. Rather, the average Aries is intrinsically disposed towards systemic maintenance, peppered with a dash of vanity. Aries are aware of foods that in excess make them feel or look bad, and they will rarely eat these or any foods beyond the level of appetite appeasement. They like an occasional rich dessert or thick steak—but only occasionally.

Essentially Aries are snackers rather than diners. They have a fundamental impatience with drawn-out meal periods, and they prefer to stay just a little lean and hungry, in case someone has a spontaneous social notion to eat. Their favorite menu category is appetizers, small and savory portions of first courses.

Although food consumption is rarely the primary focus of an Aries life, one should not discount the Aries' keen interest in matters of culinary experimentation and the even stronger appreciation for dining as a realm of social interaction (read: partying). An Aries is very happy to be at table holding forth in congenial company, although the truth is that the Aries prefers to hold first, and the company can sometimes resent their role as extras.

Thus, Aries sometimes alienate family and friends with the sheer strength of their unquenchable personal exuberance. But they sure do know how to have a good time—and they're the very best when it comes to thawing out frosty iceboxes or relations.

How do you decide to try a restaurant you've never been to before?

I'm looking for something new. Monument restaurants that serve s— food are just a colossal rip-off.

How preoccupied are you with the subjects of food and dining?

I don't eat just to eat. I have to have hunger. The food tastes much better then.

Ten Foods an Aries Needs to Survive on a Deserted Island

Bread • Fish • Cheese • Butter • Chicken
Iced tea • Fresh fruit • Coffee • Wine • Milk

What ten foods would you need to survive on a deserted island?

That's a lot. Three would be easier. Definitely coffee for medicinal purposes.

Coca-Cola. The real one. The first.

Chickens. I love to carve 'em.

No f— salad.

Aries Island

Aries like to live where the man-made environment is a springboard into the natural. Always happy adventuring out of doors, an Aries can live as contentedly in a trailer as in a palace, provided there is easy access to forests, mountains, beaches and groves—and as long as there is some ram-charged vehicle in the driveway for attacking the compass.

Actually, one of Aries' most glaring anti-social flaws is their often total lack of consideration for others when it comes to vehicular operation. Aries have a tendency to view all of life as a noisy daredevil race. This is their island, though, so let's grant them a boom town in the Klondike, with all of the Canadian and Alaskan wilderness to tool around in. Let's also throw in a reliable garage, a first-rate rescue service and a good hospital.

To be fair, one does encounter a few quiet Aries who like nothing better than to lie around on a hot beach sipping iced tea. These half-naked specimens are, however, actually generating a sort of engine heat of their own, and are quite capable of influencing the local traffic patterns.

Ultimately, someone will get run over.

The dining and food shopping environments on Aries Island are marked by informality, but they also pulse with interpersonal promise. Klondike saloons and open-air beachfront bars are part of the mix, but so are all manner of clubs, ethnic restaurants, fast food malls—any sort of establishment that might fall under the banner of "the latest hot thing." While the food in these places is of some concern, Aries primarily seek environments that engender lively and creative encounters.

Although time requirements will most often lead them to the neighborhood store for groceries, Aries are happiest shopping, because of the hum and bustle, in large markets of the Seattle Pike Street or Philadelphia Reading Terminal variety. Such a site is usually more of an outing than a shopping destination, however, and an Aries may return from such a place with a happy heart but precious few groceries.

What at first glance seem to be missing from Aries Island are formal centers of commerce, such as are found in the downtown of any legitimate city. It's not that Aries don't like to work—their aggressive energies and mania for self-assertion are amply suited to the marketplace—but their drives are usually entrepreneurial rather than organizational. Even when part of a large organization they prefer to be the ones going *mano a mano* in the field, selling and executing, as opposed to hanging around headquarters administrating and planning.

Aries therefore make wonderful foremen, military captains, sales reps, restaurant managers and executive chefs. If Aries Island didn't require so many restaurants for the inhabitants' social needs, they would have to be there as places for the population to work. Something's got to get them off the roads occasionally.

What's important to you in the evaluation of a restaurant?

Atmosphere is everything.

What's your favorite condiment?

"You look mahvelous!"

Aries Favorites

Vegetable: anything green
Fruit: peaches, strawberries, bananas
Starch: bread
Source of protein: fish, cheese
Bread product: French sourdough
Dairy product: butter
Spice or herb: pepper, cinnamon
Condiment: mustard
Ice cream flavor: mint chocolate chip
Pizza topping: loaded, often
   vegetarian with anchovies
Candy: Butterfingers
Cookie: shortbread

Sandwich: healthful turkey,
   cheeseburgers
Soup: Chinese hot and sour
Soft drink: iced tea
Beer: Heineken in bottles, Bud Light
Wine: full-bodied, flavorful
Liquor: Not usually interested; some
   bourbon, gin & tonic
Liqueur: whatever is currently "in"
Comfort food: ice cream, yogurt
Celebration food: rich dessert
Junk food: Cheez-Its
Sexy food: wine

What's your favorite protein?

Fish or turkey usually, but lately I've had a thing with lamb.

What's your favorite herb or spice?

It changes all the time.

What's your favorite celebration food?

When I'm up I don't need to eat.

Aries Diet and Health

Aries are rarely conscientious dieters, nor do they often subscribe to the "thou shalts" and "thou shalt nots" of the nutritional savants. In fact, a major health hazard for Aries would seem to be too much self-discipline or denial. The Aries inner voice says "go for it," and this is a call that must be heeded, even at the price of a few extra pounds or an occasional bout with exhaustion.

Even so, one does not come across very many overweight or sickly Aries. As a group, Aries are the most action-prone people in the zodiac, and there are few of them who don't run, swim, row, climb, dance or engage in some other form of regular athletic activity. Looking good, feeling good and performing well require that the Aries heed the inner voice about nutrition.

"Go for fish and dairy proteins more than red meat," says the inner voice.
"Eat lots of fresh fruit and vegetables, and avoid too many rich desserts."
"Select whole grain complex carbohydrates, and limit sugar and salt."

"Drink a lot of liquids, but avoid too many stimulants and intoxicants."

Of course, this is the sort of advice that would even satisfy the exacting nutritional standards of a Virgo. Sometimes, in fact, when an Aries gets on a temporary vegetarian or vitamin supplement kick, they can be mistaken for one of the zodiac's more self-denying signs. It usually won't be too long, however, before the Aries' true self shines through, because that Aries inner voice has one other rule it frequently likes to invoke:

"Party!"

Do you ever diet? How?

That's a hard question. You mean like eat cottage cheese and celery? The bottom line is: not really. I say I do.

I haven't been on a real diet that lasted more than an afternoon.

Yeah, every summer in the restaurant's kitchen—500-degree stoves and eighteen-hour days. I should write a book: *Tie Yourself to a Stove and Lose Fifty Pounds.*

Do you have any personal nutritional beliefs or habits?

I don't take all that too seriously. If they said chocolate was cancerous, I wouldn't stop eating it.

You should have a snack at 10 a.m. and 3 p.m.

Ten More Foods Most Aries Like a Whole Lot

Pasta • Potatoes • Legumes • Raw vegetables • Yogurt • Ice cream Shortbread • Beer • Coca-Cola • Roasted meat on the bone

Things You Should Not Feed an Aries

Outdated dishes
Burned, bitter or under-cooked garlic

Aries Homefood

Aries children are the ones who almost never seem to be satisfied with what is served at the dinner table. Everything is too bland and mushy, or tasteless and tough. Everything is the same.

It's not just the menu, of course. It's having to sit down, mind one's manners and slowly chew one's food. From early infancy, it is the mealtime requirement of restraint that drives an Aries wild, and they would often rather kick up a nasty fuss than take the easy route of compliance—they like going to their room, they like going anywhere.

Throughout their lives, a sort of naive impatience remains the hallmark of an Aries' domestic culinary habits. Never the best of planners, an Aries usually fails to link shopping strategy with the eventual requirements of hunger and taste. The only items guaranteed to be stocked in the Aries refrigerator are something to drink and plenty of ice.

All of this comes particularly to the fore when Aries tackle the cooking chores. Words that Aries frequently use to describe their cooking efforts are "creative," "inventive," and "experimental." Often this means that there is really nothing in the house to cook but Aries will save the day by whipping up something wonderful on the spur of the moment from the nothing on hand.

Sometimes wonderful: yes, frequently wonderful: no.

Even when an Aries cooks according to a plan there is a tendency towards abandonment of work in progress, as the Aries gets caught up in some new distraction. Aries will absentmindedly turn off a flame in the middle of a cooking process if they suddenly decide to make a phone call, or watch a favorite TV show, or run in circles around the backyard. The sometimes short attention span also leads to burning and boiling over.

Interestingly, while most Aries women profess some interest in practicing the culinary arts, most Aries men consider the duties of the kitchen to pertain to the feminine realm. The one great exception is backyard barbecuing, and no one can char like an Aries man. Or incinerate, if it comes to that.

What one almost invariably finds on an Aries kitchen shelf is, fortunately enough, a copy of *The Joy of Cooking*. Sadly, this excellent culinary reference is often brought forth as first-aid rather than preventive maintenance. Mostly it's there because Aries like the title.

Was your mother a good cook?

No. She stopped when I was twelve and went macrobiotic. She nearly killed us all.

Do you like to cook? Why?

Un huh. Because you can create something and have instant gratification.

No. By the time I'm finished cooking, I've eaten the thing out of the pot. By the time I'm done, I can't remember what the point is.

Aries Breakfast

If all the Aries in the world really lived together on the same island, the best time to see the place would be at dawn. The Aries environment is incredibly busy by daybreak, with the legion of early-rising Aries bustling along like a 33-1/3 record being played at 78. Joggers, cars, school buses, delivery trucks, chimney smoke and sunlight all stream forth from their confinements and careen down their causeways.

Oh how Aries are made for the new day!

An Aries can sometimes see breakfast as a time impediment to getting the jump. Such Aries will profess they do not much like the morning meal, although they are still quite likely to pick up some coffee on the way to work and at least to grab a mid-morning snack. Usually, though, whatever the level of personal enjoyment derived from breakfast foodstuffs, Aries value breakfast as the essential meal of the day.

For one thing, Aries are vitally aware of the relationship of food to energy. Food and oxygen are the body's fuels, and one must put something in the tank before starting out. Aries will sometimes even be content to breakfast upon foods like leftover pizza or chocolate mousse, as long as they get the motor revving.

Normally, though, Aries just like breakfast and breakfast foods, both at home and in restaurants, simply because they are associated with the freshness of morning.

Aries are more capable of realizing ecstasy at the start of the day than at any other time—if not with the companion of their dreams, then perhaps with some fruit and yogurt.

Who is your favorite companion at breakfast?

It doesn't make a difference. I'm wide awake and ready to go. If you want to talk, I'm ready to talk.

What do you generally eat for lunch during the work week?

I don't usually eat lunch if I have breakfast. If I eat breakfast I often don't eat again until the next morning.

What's your favorite restaurant anywhere? Why?

I can't decide. The Good Egg. I love their breakfast food. Everything else is too elegant.

Aries Breakfast Favorites

Juices: grapefruit, tropical blend
Fruit: chilled melon
Cereal: nutritional flakes with sliced fruit
Sweet rolls: pecan rolls, raisin buns
Bread: whole wheat toast
Egg dish: poached or omelet with vegetables
Others: whole wheat and fruit pancakes with maple syrup; yogurt and
   healthful toppings

Aries Awayfood

There are lots of reasons for eating out that have to do with serious things like time and money and the pursuit of quality. There are also many serious ways of evaluating a restaurant experience, paying attention to such factors as culinary performance, service caliber and rest room cleanliness, for example. An Aries is not necessarily unconcerned about such things.

To an Aries, however, there is one dining quality that almost invariably takes precedence, whether one speaks of patron intent or restaurant execution. An Aries must have this to consider a dining experience successful. Without it there is no real achievement; with it the greatest flaw in value or performance may be overlooked.

Ultimately, an Aries just wants to have fun.

Certainly, even for Aries, "fun" is not a monochromatic concept. An Aries' list of favorite restaurants is likely to include a broad range of places, from California bistros to great seafood houses, neighborhood fern bars, private clubs, breakfast pantries, local ethnic joints and fast food establishments; and an Aries' dining purposes will be as diverse as those of the natives of any other astrological sign.

Yet there is a link between Aries' favorite dining establishments and certain enjoyable experiences, which may be mutually described in terms of novelty, warmth, casualness, decency, freshness, amiability and general ease of appreciation. Aries always favor a place in which something upbeat and spontaneous may occur. But they do not react well when they are challenged by an environment, be it with formality, fierceness, funkiness or even too much fun.

Of course, what is really the most fun for Aries is any sort of scouting expedition, and their very favorite restaurants may be simply characterized as "new." Most people try a place because it has been recommended to them.

Aries try a restaurant because it has just opened—and, conversely, will abandon one simply because it has become too well-known.

Likewise, as for specific cuisines, Aries will be the first to try Cajun or sushi or Thai food, and the first to abandon them when they are discovered by everyone else. Their menu preferences run towards appetizers, snacks and other small portions of savories, the sustenance of the sampler as opposed to the main-course musings of the serious diner. They are definitely put off by chefs and cuisines that take themselves too seriously, and they expect to be handed the ketchup without comment if that is their desire of the moment.

Understandably, Aries can sometimes be found in the midst of a restaurant ruckus, either as the customer who demands a well-done filet or the chef who demands it be eaten rare. Aries are also not smooth when it comes to dealing with service personnel (it's hard for an Aries to show much self-restraint around someone who has to accept the Aries directives), and they are notoriously poor tippers (paying extra for attention does not compute).

More often, though, an Aries is just the person in a restaurant obviously having fun. More often.

What's your favorite restaurant anywhere? Why?

> Julio's La Corona Cafe in Juarez, Mexico. The food is simple, it hasn't changed since the restaurant opened in the '30s. They knew about cilantro before anyone else. The place is so Mexican—stucco rooms, bright colors, just trashy enough. They don't think about it, they just do it.

What's your favorite restaurant entrée?

> Either frog's legs or rabbit because I've never had them. I love to experiment.

Romantic Menus for Aries

To romance him:

Table: backyard picnic table or blanket
Appetizer: vegetable tempura with hot mustard dipping sauce
Salad: tossed greens with gorgonzola dressing
Bread: plain biscuits and sweet butter
Entrée: barbecue ribs and shrimp; corn on the cob; watermelon
Beverage: premium bottled beer
Dessert: warm pecan pie and vanilla ice cream; coffee

To romance her:

Table: bright solid colors, especially reds, oranges and greens
Appetizer: baked oysters Rockefeller
Soup: tomato crab bisque
Bread: crusty French rolls and sweet butter
Entrée: grilled salmon and cilantro butter; curried vegetables
Wine: Mosel Kabinett
Dessert: Baked Alaska; cappuccino

Aries Food Fantasy

Hans Christian Andersen had it about right. Aries' fantasies are of princes and princesses—of heroic actions boldly undertaken and richly rewarded—of triumphant parties.

In real life, Aries ram head first into all sorts of obstacles. In their dreams, they are perfect navigators. Bat smart. Instinctive. Spontaneous and lucky.

There is another sort of Aries fantasy, though, and in some ways it is a deeper kind. It is Aries' fantasy about what they are usually incapable of managing, even in their dreams. Ultimately, Aries fantasize about relaxation.

There is a warm cozy room with a fireplace.

There may be a lover and a bottle of wine. There may be family with turkey, mashed potatoes and gravy. There may be friends with fresh peaches and a bag of Lorna Doones.

And all the frogs are princes, and all the ugly ducklings are swans, and everyone is peaceful and content and living happily ever after.

Still, you ask Aries about fantasies and they'll choose reality most every time. Their last meal would be something like a burger and a beer. They would be celebrating life's adventures and honest pleasures, never really believing that there is something like an ultimate pay-off or goal.

Even if there is a better life beyond, most Aries would prefer to get there by four-wheel drive. To Aries, heaven is actually a great tailgate party.

What would be your idea of the perfect meal?

In Hawaii. No, no, no, scratch that. In Italy, or Spain, or France, probably on the water. South of France. An outdoor cafe. A nice bottle of wine, light salad with a vinaigrette dressing. Do I need to be specific? Any broiled fish, halibut with light sauce, pasta, peas and carrots, glazed baby carrots, French ice cream for dessert with cappuccino. More wine.

Just wine.

Polenta with Cheese and Chiles

submitted by Laurie Vacha

1-1/2 cups chicken stock
1-1/2 cups polenta (Italian-style cornmeal)
1-1/2 cups grated parmesan cheese
2 jalapeño peppers, seeded and chopped

Bring stock to boil and gradually stir in polenta. Reduce heat and continue stirring for 5 minutes. Add cheese and chiles and remove from heat. Spoon into 4" x 8" loaf pan immediately. Let stand for 30 minutes to firm. Run a knife around the edge of pan and turn polenta out onto board. Cut crosswise into eight slices; cut diagonally in half. Brown slices in lightly buttered pan and serve with sour cream.

Pad Thai

submitted by Desiree Witkowski

1/2 lb. Thai rice noodles
1/2 cup oil
1 T. white vinegar
2 T. fish sauce
1/2 t. paprika
1 egg

1/4 cup peeled and cleaned shrimp, soaked in hot water
1 T. sugar
2 cups bean sprouts
2 green onions, cut into 2" lengths
2-1/2 T. ground roasted peanuts

Soak noodles in cold water 10-15 minutes until slightly soft. Heat 1/3 cup oil in wok. Add drained noodles and stir-fry quickly. Add vinegar, fish sauce and paprika and stir.

Push noodles to one side of wok. Pour a little oil next to noodles. Break egg into oil and cook without scrambling until almost firm. Break up egg and stir in noodles. Add drained shrimp, sugar, bean sprouts and green onions and stir. Stir in heaping tablespoon of crushed peanuts. Turn noodles out onto serving platter and top with remaining peanuts.

Curried Chicken Salad

submitted by Claudia Cumsky

2 cups cubed, cooked chicken
2 large celery stalks, thinly sliced
1/4 cup slivered almonds
1/4 cup raisins
1 medium green onion, thickly
    sliced
2 T. mango chutney

Dressing:
3 T. mayonnaise
1 T. curry powder
1 T. Dijon mustard
1 t. fresh lemon juice
1 large clove minced garlic

Mix chicken, vegetables and chutney. Blend dressing ingredients, then combine with chicken mixture. Serve on a bed of lettuce with fruit around it and it's spectacular.

Peanut Butter on a Cucumber

submitted by Roger VonSpiegel

It's my specialty. Use the chunky kind.

Toll House Cookies

submitted by Gael Hartford

Get it off the Nestlé's bag.

Scotch Shortbread

submitted by Elaine Johnson

1 lb. butter
1 cup sugar
4 cups all-purpose flour
1 cup rice flour (rice flour is good because it makes it crunchy.)

Beat butter and sugar until smooth. Add all-purpose flour and rice flour, a cup at a time, and mix until smooth—you'll probably have to use your hands.

    Pat into a jelly roll pan and bake in a 275° oven for 1 hour, until golden. Cut in pieces while warm; sprinkle with granulated sugar and let cool in pan.

Strawberries Kelly Ann

submitted by Robert A. Schafer

1 lb. fresh strawberries, stemmed
1 cup sour cream
1/2 cup brown sugar
1/4 cup Amaretto

Wash and quarter strawberries. In a large balloon wine glass place 1 oz. of sour cream and sprinkle with 1/2 oz. (1 tablespoon) of brown sugar. Sprinkle 4 oz. of the quartered strawberries on top of the sour cream/brown sugar. Place another 1 oz. of sour cream on top of the strawberries and sprinkle another 1/2 oz. of brown sugar over the top of the sour cream. Repeat in three other wine glasses.

Place in refrigerator until ready to be served, then pour 1/2 oz. of Amaretto over the top and serve with a chilled spoon. Serves four.

Some Aries Food Personalities

Phyllis Richman, executive food editor, *Washington Post*
Bradley Ogden, executive chef, Campton Place, San Francisco

Taurus

April 20 to May 21

There is absolutely no substitute for the best. Good food cannot be made of inferior ingredients masked with high flavor. It is true thrift to use the best ingredients available and to waste nothing. If you use the best butter, eggs, cream, meat and other ingredients, and use them carefully and wisely, you will have less waste than if you search for bargains and end up with a full garbage pail.

James Beard (Taurus), food authority
from *The Fireside Cookbook*

I'm not totally preoccupied with food. But it's right up there with sex and baseball.

Cap'n Dave Walker (Taurus),
'gut-bomb' restaurant critic

To know the Taureans, children of the early spring, is to recognize how well the sign is suited for life on earth. The Bull is a contented denizen of the material plane, and pursues its rewards with great commitment and conviction. Success is abundance to Taurus, and nothing is more enjoyable than digging right in.

Although they often seem reserved, perhaps 'calm' is a better term, Taureans are not without a great deal of passion and power. When it comes to sensory experience they prefer pleasure on the intense side, strong and lasting. Taurus is enamored of good things that take their own sweet time.

When it comes to food and dining, such attributes are first translated into very strong opinions about quality. Taurus rejects the cheap, the fast and the faddish in favor of the classic, the carefully-crafted and the sublime. Possessed of finely-tuned palates, and often talented cooks themselves, they are highly critical of food that is bland, inexpertly prepared and stylistically phonied-up.

Taureans prefer fresh and unprocessed foods. In flavors they favor earthy and mineral-rich tastes—potatoes and other root vegetables, greens, nuts, coffee, grains, dry wines, herbs, mineral water—and they are never the sort willingly to make enemies of salt and sugar. (Perhaps the most intriguing American culinary event of the late 20th century was Taurean James Beard's being placed on a salt-restricted diet—and the commotion about alternative seasoning methods that ensued. If the truth be told, however, there's plenty of salt in Mr. Beard's later recipe collections. Or instead of placing salt on a baked potato, he substitutes caviar).

The real food "problem" that confronts Taurus is that in addition to natural earthy-tasting flavors, the Bull also likes food that is rich. There is no bigger fan of butter, cream cheese, ice cream and eggs. And there are an awful lot of red meat-'n'-tater Taureans who seem almost totally oblivious of the claims made against cholesterol.

Where this really starts to cause some damage is in the esteem the average Taurus grants both pleasure and abundance. Sometimes a Taurus will turn towards shopping or investments or even a real lover. Just as frequently, though, an attachment will be made to the refrigerator door.

Still, if Taurus is sometimes deservedly chastised for self-indulgence, the Bull may also be envied for it. For no one gets a bigger or more discerning kick out of the pleasures of the earth, not the least of which is a good dinner.

Select a family holiday in which food plays an important part. Name it and briefly describe the food.

Christmas. Turkey and dressing; pickles and olives; cranberry sauce; bibb lettuce with avocado and pink grapefruit slices; creamed onions; baked oysters; Christmas cookies; toffee bars; tree and wreath shapes; thumbprints with cherry centers; Frango Mints from Marshall Field's; squash; champagne; salted nuts; homemade vanilla ice cream; fruit cake garnished with holly sprig.

What new trends on the restaurant scene don't you like?

I don't like all these diners. The food is too bland.

What's a celebration food?

Filet mignon, scampi, scallops, French bread, two wines, a good dessert and me. What else could you want?

Ten Foods a Taurus Needs to Survive on a Deserted Island

Beef • Chocolate • Mineral water • Orchard fruit • Salad greens
Bread and butter • Milk or cream • Potatoes • Eggs • Cheese

What ten foods and/or beverages would you want on a deserted island?

We're talking good quality stuff.

I'm getting all turned on talking about this. If you had me over for steak, lobster and champagne, I'd marry you.

Taurus Island

There's not a single fast food restaurant in sight on Taurus Island. There may *be* a few fast food restaurants, but they won't be easy to pick out in the landscape. For even if Taureans will occasionally patronize such establishments—Taureans are very sensitive to factors of price/value and in certain cases they even sort of like the food—they certainly don't want to *look* at the places all of the time.

Matters of aesthetics, durability, purpose and pleasure are always considered in the Taurus environment. Taureans can claim many architects, builders, developers, farmers, gardeners and sculptors among their ranks, and their island is an agreeable tribute to talent and taste united. Taureans build as if they are going to be around a long time and intend to appreciate things while they're here.

Not unexpectedly, Taureans are often collectors of fine art and other luxury assets. Home and office interiors are often utilized to create suitable environments in which to display these collections. Taureans go for this look in restaurants—white-washed walls and starched white linens, natural light in daytime and mellow glows at midnight, fresh flowers and simple yet expensive appointments, a few works of fine art—all suitable background for cuisine almost beyond praise and nearly good enough to forget about the expense.

Taurus' devoted patronage of quality is reflected in the island's considerable number of expensive galleries and shops. Interestingly, many of the stores are large rather than quaint—Taureans go for fancy department stores and superior quality supermarkets—because Taureans love picking out the best from among a wide array of the merely better. Even if they just need to pick up something in a hurry, they want to shop at a place where the existence of quality items is assured.

Sometimes, all this shopping means that dinner will be furnished from a drive-through. But don't even think of suggesting such a place for a date. On Taurus Island, that would be a mistake out of all proportion.

What's your favorite fast food?

I sometimes go through the Jack-in-the-Box drive-through. I wear dark glasses, a raincoat and hold the newspaper in front of my face.

How preoccupied are you with the subjects of food and dining?

I'm more of a materialist than a foodie. I'd rather have a fabulous purse or a new dress, and I'll give up food to get it.

Taurus Favorites

Vegetable: broccoli
Fruit: berries, apples
Starch: potatoes with skins
Source of protein: beef
Bread product: croissants, rye
Dairy product: milk
Spice or herb: garlic, basil
Condiment: Russian dressing
Ice cream flavor: Neapolitan
Pizza topping: pepperoni
Candy: chocolate fudge
Cookie: chewy chocolate chip

Sandwich: pastrami-turkey-Swiss
 on rye
Soup: vegetable beef
Soft drink: mineral water
Beer: Budweiser
Wine: earthy reds
Liquor: premium Scotch
Liqueur: Amaretto
Comfort food: pizza and beer
Celebration food: lasagna
Junk food: don't like the term "junk"
Sexy food: lobster; berries and cream

What's your favorite candy?

Blackcurrant pastilles. That's twenty-seven bucks on Madison Avenue.

What's your favorite alcoholic beverage?

Champagne. Good champagne. Not the cheap stuff.

What's your favorite liquor?

Chivas on the rocks, which isn't cheap either.

What's your favorite soup?

Fresh cream of mushroom. I don't eat canned.

What's a sexy food?

Food is really important and sensual to Taureans. I once made love in chicken salad.

Taurus Diet and Health

Fundamentally, Taureans are sensualists. So even if they sincerely understand and try to practice the virtues of moderation and regularity, they are always capable of unbridled feats of consumption. They are also capable of astounding feats of restraint—but the Taurus nature runs decidedly towards acquisition.

When the Taurus sensual nature is aroused and food is made its object, the ingestion can become legendary. The Taurus will then treat a package as a portion—a portion of bread is a loaf, of drink a bottle, of doughnuts or eggs a dozen—and the whole menu as a meal. Sometimes Taureans have to keep their houses empty of groceries, because these are the people who will compensate for dissatisfaction in other material areas by eating everything that isn't nailed down.

Compounding the way-above-average caloric intake is the Taurean tendency towards inertia. Once they get into something enjoyable to their senses, they are not eager to rush to a conclusion and get into something else. And, as has already been mentioned, they are much more likely to get hooked on cream cheese than cauliflower (although they will happily spread some cream cheese on this as well).

At least nature has seen fit to help the situation by endowing Taurus with a strong constitution. If they are into physical culture, as many Taureans are, their generally protein-rich diet helps to develop a lot of muscle. Taureans are fond of serious body-building and are frequently found herded around the power and endurance equipment in the gym.

One does encounter some lean and lithe Taureans, but these people are frequently into the sensuality of denial. They are Taureans for someone else's book.

What's your favorite bread?

Whole wheat with raisins. I love this. I eat it a loaf at a time.

Do you ever diet? How?

> Instead of dieting I'm more of a supply-sider. I'd rather work out than restrict intake.

> I believe behavior modification is the best diet. But it's easier said than done.

Do you have any personal nutritional beliefs or habits?

> I believe certain foods can give you a more stable mind and bring inner peace. The four food groups bring inner stability to you.

> Budweiser.

Ten More Foods Most Taureans Like a Whole Lot

Tomatoes • Butter • Carrots • Bagels with cream cheese • Nuts
Chicken • Tuna • Seafood • Red wine • Salads

Things You Should Not Feed a Taurus

Overcooked herbs and vegetables
Inferior-quality ingredients
Mint-flavored foods

What are some foods or flavors that turn you off?

> Anise, okra, poi, camebert cheese, liver, tripe, boiled tongue, menudo, anchovies, anchovies and more anchovies.

Taurus Homefood

Taureans are strongly invested in their living spaces. A home, to Taurus, is the truest measure of a person's taste, durability and wealth of spirit. It is a powerful realm of status and responsibility, and it is also a den of the deepest comforts and pleasures.

Taurus often adopts the role of guardian of the home. Even if commuting breadwinners, Taurus will always find time to make essential repairs, tend the garden, write the checks, stock the pantry and, above all else, to make sure that everything and everyone are safe and secure. Taurus tends towards over-protectiveness, and friends are advised not to barge in unexpectedly because "the door was unlocked."

In the kitchen, Taureans are usually among the best of cooks because of compatible qualities of diligence and talent. They are truly knowledgeable and creative without being wildly experimental. They understand a lot about the variable dynamics of timing, texture and taste, and what they do they do excellently.

Taureans love to touch, and they love cooking that involves a great deal of product handling. A particular pleasure is sticking their fingers in a pot to taste and see how things are progressing. Bread making, with all its kneading, punching, braiding, brushing, is a particular delight to Taureans, who are also much charmed by a good aromatic symphony.

Like most people nowadays, Taureans find less time to cook. Still, their deliberate and painstaking natures gives them a special affinity for recipes requiring lengthy and scrupulous preparation. They particularly like the important family holidays and their attendant roasts, vegetable casseroles, crafted desserts and elaborately designed buffets.

Of course, Taurus also likes special occasions as they afford an opportunity for the Bull to show off the good china. Even more deeply, though, Taureans enjoy sharing quality experiences with the people they love. Much like a singer with a great voice, practiced talent and a repertoire of timeless classics, the Taurus cook/host/entertainer/parent is adept at pleasing everyone by pleasing himself or herself—it is a serene and secure situation.

Do you like to cook?

I love to cook as long as someone enjoys eating it. It brings a lot of pleasure and satisfaction.

Was your mother a good cook?

Mmm...hmm, but I didn't like her fried round steak with ketchup and onions. Ugh.

Taurus Breakfast

Taureans have a fairly mellow morning attitude. Inclined to take the long view of a day, they don't ordinarily wake up with a lot of nervous energy or a huge amount of reticence about getting down to work. They will usually take their time about getting into any fixed attitude (once there it will keep), and mostly enjoy morning for its gentle rustlings, its note of fresh optimism and its familiar flavors and smells.

Taureans truly love coffee and toast as much for their aroma as for their flavor. They also love the tastes and textures of cereal products, the sweetness of fruit, the saltiness of breakfast meats and the richness of doughnuts and other morning pastries. And of course the Bull loves just about anything that comes from a cow.

If circumstances place Taureans outside the home for breakfast, they enjoy charismatic company as well as a good feed. Taureans are perfectly suited for the power breakfast, and have no trouble discussing value over a good meal. They will not, however, reach snap decisions about truly important issues without some rumination (and further discussion over a power lunch).

The Taurus is very fond of the bounty of a good Sunday brunch, but the real morning glory for Taurus the sensualist is breakfast in bed. Champagne, fresh orange juice, imported salmon, charismatic company, sweet stuff and so on. And on.

Who would be an ideal fantasy companion for breakfast?

Adolf Hitler.

Ronald Reagan.

PeeWee Herman.

Time and a beautiful view.

O mama, I'd sell my mother for breakfast with Mickey Rourke. He's awesome.

What do you generally eat for breakfast during the work week?

Coffee and aspirin.

Who would be an ideal fantasy companion for lunch?

Harry Hamlin and chicken salad.

Taurus Breakfast Favorites

Juices: fresh fruit nectars, peach juice and champagne
Fruit: fresh berries with cream
Cereal: hot cereals with brown sugar, butter and cream; Chex
Sweet rolls: whole wheat raisin nut muffins
Bread: bagels with cream cheese; croissants
Egg dish: fluffy omelet with herbed cheese filling; fried with country ham
Other: pecan waffles with butter and maple syrup; bacon; salmon

Taurus Awayfood

As the culinary clock passes on from the historical moment of *nouvelle cuisine*, it is worth honoring some of the movement's real achievements. The creators and practitioners of this exalted culinary style have re-taught us to enjoy such virtues as freshness, lightness, naturalness, purity and, perhaps above all else, elegant simplicity in our dining. A true aesthetic has been developed, based on artistic vision, awareness of historical culinary technique and tradition, a superb understanding of cooking principles and the properties of taste, and an immense commitment to the quality of ingredients available and performance possible.

Nobody, but nobody, appreciates material quality and well-rendered artistic vision more than Taureans, and they love *nouvelle* and *oldsville cuisine* done with value and distinction. They can even be as fond of great junk food as they are of the fancy stuff, provided it's really great junk food. When Taureans rave about a little hole in the wall somewhere, they are definitely to be trusted.

Special restaurant food favorites include fine wines, prime beef and seafood, large salads, warm bread, rich desserts and just about any food eaten with the hands. The person at the table who is eating a salad with his fingers may not be an insensitive boor but, rather, a sensual bull. They are also the sort whose hands can be quite active under the table.

Taureans usually favor a broad selection on a menu, but they do not like elaborate or cute description. They want effort put into cooking, not copywriting. Even when the menu is brief, however, a Taurus will generally be cautious and deliberate in selection—there is, after all, an art to composing a meal.

Sometimes a Taurus can seem impossibly deliberate, and pity the waiter who tries to speed up the act. Taurus can and will out-wait anyone. If the waiter manages to provoke anger, the best tip he'll get is to disappear.

Taureans have a particularly strong need to be physically comfortable in a restaurant, and they will be very aware of such diverse matters as room temperature, traffic and ventilation flows, the shape of the chairs and the contribution of staff uniforms and the dining room mural to overall ambience. They seek environmental harmony and find it hard to luxuriate when elements clash.

Not much, though, spoils their appetites.

What new trends on the restaurant scene don't you like?

> A turn-off is all the restaurateurs who hop on the latest bandwagon; people who just throw money at the new trends.

What's important to you in the evaluation of a restaurant?

I like to hear specific detail. If someone says "the food is lousy," that doesn't help me. But if they say they got their medium steak served well-done, I have an idea about it.

Do you prefer to eat out or to eat at home?

It depends on the situation. You can get a better and more economical meal out sometimes. I go out and eat by myself nicely. I do it all the time. I'm not shy.

Romantic Menus for Taurus

To romance him:

Table: wrought iron candlesticks, pewter, heavy utensils; warm bread and
      butter
Appetizer: beer cheese soup
Salad: good green salad with herbed buttermilk dressing
Entrée: chateaubriand with sauce bordelaise; mushroom caps; duchesse
      potatoes ; glazed carrots; parsley (Taureans like to *eat* parsley)
Wine: the best dry red wine your budget will allow
Dessert: rich chocolate cake with whipped cream and chocolate shavings;
      dessert port and freshly brewed coffee

To romance her:

Table: exquisite understatement; fresh flowers in crystal
Appetizer: French onion soup with melted gruyère; chilled Amontillado
      sherry
Salad: bibb, watercress with creamy vinaigrette
Entrée: lobster tails and sliced sirloin; fettucini Alfredo; broccoli almandine
Wine: any *expensive* fine quality wine
Dessert: cheesecake with fresh berry sauce; tea

Taurus Food Fantasy

Taurus fantasies deserve to be expressed as art. They are sensual enough to stimulate rapture and lovely enough to break hearts. They are real enough to be universally recognizable and privately cherished.

So much is revealed in Taurean desire because the Bull is almost incapable of deception. Taureans are what they seem to be and their secret wishes, even when not articulated, are very close to the surface. Taureans, even in their deepest desires, deal with those things which can be made manifest in the material world.

So it is that any Taurean would love to be served an exquisite meal in a great hotel suite—a special friend, a champagne breakfast, a satin comforter and flannel sheets. Napoleon in ruins in the whirlpool tub.

So it is that any Taurean would love to throw an unforgettable party for friends—Bruce Springsteen at Wrigley Field, Barbra Streisand at Cartier's. Either way a great buffet.

So it is that any Taurean would love to enjoy any particularly fine food in any particularly exquisite environment with any particularly compelling view and any particularly sweet company. Masters of the material. Sages of sensuality.

What may be most revealing about them, though, is the most common of Taurean food fantasies. There is a prime rib or roast turkey, a nice green salad, vegetable casseroles and ice cream—a family holiday with lots of affection and plenty of time.

Lots and plenty of everything.

What would be your idea of the perfect meal?

> This is impossible. It depends on too many things. I'll say tea with scones at Claridges in London with my mother after a day of shopping at Harrods at Christmas time. Or champagne and dim sum with a small group of my best friends and family at an elegant private party in San Francisco. Or fresh-squeezed orange juice and blueberry pancakes on the patio of a restaurant on Nantucket Island in early September with a special friend.

Carrot Pudding

submitted by Mona Weisman

1/4 cup margarine
1/2 cup brown sugar
2 eggs
2 cups mashed cooked carrots
1 cup flour

1 t. baking powder
1/2 t. salt
1/2 t. baking soda
1/4 cup orange juice

Mix all ingredients together. Pour into greased 8" square pan. Bake at 350° for 45 minutes.

Marilyn's Pasta Salad

submitted by Ralph Ribicia

1/4 lb. salami, cut in strips
1 pint cooked noodles
2 pints broccoli florets
1/4 cup pine nuts
1 small can sliced olives
1/2 red onion, sliced
1/2 red bell pepper, sliced

Dressing:
1/2 cup oil
1/2 cup vinegar
1 t. thyme
1/2 t. oregano
2 cloves garlic
1 t. salt
1/4 cup fresh basil (or 2 T. dry)

Combine salami, noodles, nuts and vegetables. Cover and place in refrigerator. Blend dressing ingredients and pour over pasta salad.

The Elvis

submitted by Dave Walker

It's a fried egg sandwich with cheese and mayo.

Heavenly Potatoes

submitted by Janna Partilla-Trout

15 potatoes
1 onion, grated
1 cup melted butter
1/2 pint whipping cream

1 pint half and half
salt, white pepper and paprika
to taste

Day 1: Parboil potatoes 20 minutes. Cool, refrigerate. Day 2: Peel potatoes and grate into a shallow 3-quart casserole. Mix onions as little as possible. Pour butter, cream and half and half over potatoes. Season to taste and stir gently. Cover and chill. Day 3: Remove casserole 2 hours before baking. Sprinkle with paprika. Bake at 325° for 1 hour. Serves twelve to sixteen.

Brisket

submitted by Peggy Feinman

Take a brisket fat-side up; put it in a roast pan. Lawry's seasoned salt and pepper both sides. Put Lipton onion soup on top. Slice a whole onion on top of that. Mix one part ketchup to one part water and pour on top of brisket. Cover and cook at 250° for 8 hours. Take out; let cool. Slice, cover and put overnight in the refrigerator. Next day, re-heat and serve.

Chicken en Croute

submitted by Tina Wilcox

8 Pillsbury crescent rolls
4 boneless chicken breasts
1/2 t. tarragon

1 t. lemon juice
2 T. butter
1 egg, beaten

Take roll dough and make four rectangles out of eight triangles. Flatten them out. Mix butter, lemon and tarragon into a paste. Lay chicken on rectangle spread with paste mixture. Roll up jelly roll style, making sure to cover all chicken edges. Bake 375° for 1/2 hour. Then brush with beaten egg and bake 5 minutes more until golden brown. Great cold the next day.

Filet Danny

submitted by Mark Kosanovich

6 oz. of beef tenderloin
small quantity of flour
cracked peppercorns
2 oz. Burgundy wine
1/2 cup chopped mushrooms

2 t. unsalted butter
2 t. chopped garlic
2 t. pesto
1 T. green onions, chopped
parsley

Take the filet and slice into three 2-oz. medallions. Lightly dust in flour and press in cracked peppercorns, sauté in clarified butter to degree of doneness. Set the cooked medallions on a plate and drain off excess butter from pan. Into pan add the wine, green onions, mushrooms, pesto and garlic. Reduce, then add unsalted butter while shaking sauté pan over flame and whisking sauce. Top the filet with the newly-made sauce, and garnish with parsley. Accompany dish with steamed egg linguine with marinara sauce.

Sour Cream Coffee Cake

submitted by Susan Whittier

1/2 cup butter
1/2 cup shortening
1-1/4 cups sugar
2 eggs
1 cup sour cream
1 t. vanilla extract
2 cups sifted flour
1 t. baking powder
1/2 t. baking soda

Topping:
1 cup chopped walnuts
1/4 cup sugar
1 t. cinnamon

Cream butter, shortening and sugar. Add eggs, sour cream and vanilla. Gradually add flour, baking powder and soda. In buttered, floured 9" Bundt pan, sprinkle some topping. Layer 1/3 batter, 1/4 topping, 1/3 batter, 1/4 topping, 1/3 batter, rest of topping. Bake at 350° for 1 hour. Cool 15 minutes. Remove from pan. Serve warm or cooled.

Butterscotch Nut Torte

Submitted by T. Keith Harrison.
This recipe was the first place winner in the Tennessee Egg Cooking Contest and was created by Mrs. Melba E. Wright of Winchester, Tennessee.

Torte:
6 Tennessee egg yolks
1-1/2 cups sugar
1 t. baking powder
2 t. vanilla
1 t. almond extract
6 Tennessee egg whites
2 cups graham cracker crumbs
1 cup chopped pecans
1/2 pint whipping cream, whipped

Butterscotch sauce:
1 cup brown sugar
1 T. flour
1/4 cup butter
1/4 cup orange juice
1/4 cup water
2 Tennessee eggs
1/2 t. vanilla

Torte: Beat egg yolks well; add sugar and baking powder. Add vanilla and almond flavorings. Beat egg whites until stiff, not dry. Fold in egg yolks, cracker crumbs and nuts. Pour mixture into 9-1/2" torte pan and bake at 325° oven for 35 to 40 minutes. Cool and frost with whipping cream.

Sauce: Combine sugar and flour. Add butter, orange juice, water and eggs. Cook until thick over double boiler. Add vanilla and cool. Cut torte and pour sauce over individual pieces just before serving. Serves eight.

Some Taurus Food Personalities

James Beard, cookbook author, pre-eminent American culinary authority
Connie Welch, food editor, *Weight Watchers* magazine
Gerard Pangaud, executive chef, Aurora Restaurant, New York City

Gemini

May 22 to June 21

From the thousand responses of my heart never to cease,
From the myriad thence-arous'd words,
From the word stronger and more delicious than any...

> Walt Whitman (Gemini), poet
> from "Out of the Cradle Endlessly Rocking"

In perfect dining you finish the entrée right in the very middle of the evening. Then you start communicating, talking, spending time together.

> Tom Frank (Gemini), restaurateur

If Geminis were literary devices, they would be streams of metaphors or chains of adjectives. If Geminis were food, they would be well-stocked condiment caddies or deli buffets. Always with Gemini, there is a special way with baloney.

Throughout their lives, Geminis retain the precocious and energetic intellects of young children. These people always seem to be discovering new potentials and counter-potentials of speech and thought. Attracting attention through verbal display, tirelessly altering their own perceptions and baffling everyone else with a curiously compulsive mixture of sense and nonsense are the clearly recognized hallmarks of Gemini behavior.

Although they are most often friendly, bright, witty, charming and versatile, Geminis frequently give the impression over the long haul that there is little "there" there. Mental agility and the compulsion for intellectual embellishment are so pronounced, that it is almost impossible to pin these people down about absolute belief or commitment. Now you see them, now you see something else.

In the worst cases, Geminis can be rather addicted to reality-bending (*read*: outrageous lying). To themselves they are merely demonstrating the power of mind over matter and, with their liking for "tales," they are really just attempting to rescue the world from having to accept the boredom of mundane truth. They thus come off as clever, but people who like their truth a little on the solid side often find Gemini flighty, vain, and a little un-trustworthy.

Howsoever, to Gemini the most delicious thing that can ever be placed in one's mouth is a well-prepared phrase. At gut-level, Geminis are just not that interested in food and dining. Functioning on a quick, almost nervous, men-tal frequency, Geminis generally find processes of eating and digestion to be a drag on rapid mental processing.

On the other hand, Geminis do have great fondness for the social aspects of dining, insofar as these occasions provide the opportunity for gathering and talking. It is also true that any subject may appeal to the Gemini mind, and this is no less true of food and dining than other subjects. Geminis who become hobbyists in this area, or who are captured by a food profession, are often amazingly well-read and informed about the vast trivia of the food universe and, if they are cooks, are capable of exceptionally cunning culinary performances.

Foods that do appeal to Gemini are of the small savory variety—such things as are found on deli trays, in salad bowls, in chafing dishes, in ethnic-cuisine restaurants and on appetizer menus. They are not particularly fond of large portions of any one food, as they are always looking as much for amusement as for appetite satisfaction. They generally prefer spicy to bland.

One interesting quirk of Gemini taste is a pronounced affection for round foods such as pizzas, oranges, cakes, bagels, olives, etc., which are perhaps useful food metaphors for people who have trouble reaching ultimate conclu-sions.

While they are avid consumers of "light" products, especially soda and beer, they may also occasionally over-indulge in the rich foods of childhood, such as candy, ice cream and red-sauced and cheesy Italian foods. Over-weight Geminis sometimes get that way as a response to perennial nervous exhaustion, but they are just as often manifesting some of the dining attrib-utes of Gemini's neighboring signs, Taurus and Cancer, both fairly self-indulgent food signs.

Note: People born under a given sun sign almost inevitably manifest some of the characteristics of one or both of the sun signs on either side of it. This has to do with the placement in an individual's horoscope of the various planets, particularly Mercury and Venus, which can never occur (from the earth's perspective) in a sign too far from the sign where the sun is. This may confuse more than clarify, but a Gemini has a fondness for footnotes and other addenda, so I wanted to provide one here. Actually, if a Gemini likes a footnote well enough, he or she is capable of reading an entire book on a subject, which suits me just fine.

Ultimately, if the truth of one's culinary convictions may be measured from the contents of the cupboard, Gemini is rather a flash in the pan. There may be an occasional esoteric ingredient or a few well-chosen cookbooks on the premises, but a Gemini refrigerator often contains nothing more than space and a twenty-five watt bulb. And a few cold cuts.

Do you like to cook?

I was such a lousy cook that all my friends bought me cookbooks as wedding gifts. I read them and became a pretty good cook and now I really love to give intimate dinner parties. But I'm in corporate communications so I'm not home too much to give them.

I love to cook. Because it's manic.

What's your favorite cookbook?

The Joy of Thawing.

What is there more of than anything else in your refrigerator?

Light.

Ten Foods a Gemini Needs to Survive on a Deserted Island

Salad • Condiments • Fish • Chicken • Bagels with cream cheese
Apples • Wine • Oranges • Potatoes • Pizza

What ten foods would you need to survive on a deserted island?

I'm not a sweets person, but you gotta have something sweet.

Gemini Island

Gemini Island is a cross between a school playground and the set for a wine-cooler commercial. But it's the adults who are playing on the teeter-totters, and the kids who are running around on the boulevard. Ah, sweet environmental chaos!

For all their mental vagaries, Geminis bond very closely with their neighborhoods. There is a lot to be learned by a fresh perception of even the most ordinary things, and Geminis have little trouble being stimulated by any environment in which they find themselves. As long as there's a lot of fresh air and everything's not too neat and tidy.

Perhaps the great consistency of Gemini life is the maintenance of interest in siblings, childhood friends and adolescent turf. These are the agents of early developmental awareness, and Geminis have powerful recollections of the places and people that first engender the processes of mental interaction. The real shrines of Gemini life are such places as schoolrooms, neighborhood libraries, the local park, grandma's house, the family car and fast food restaurants.

In terms of dining, Gemini Island is really a world of school cafeterias and family restaurants. The keynote is high-amplitude bustle, and everywhere there seems to be an animated group engaged in noisy, informal celebration. The dining establishments of Gemini Island all have lots of tables for large parties.

Of course, there is also a more mature side to Gemini tastes, and this is reflected in the island's numerous "light and healthful" restaurants featuring grilled seafood, salad and an interesting assortment of wines by the glass. There are also numerous specialty food shops and delis, as Geminis enjoy the mental stimulation of a treasure hunt. Geminis are particularly turned on by open-air markets with exotica-laden kiosks, but they can also be delighted by any ordinary ice cream truck or pizza joint offering a choice of several out-of-the-ordinary flavors and/or toppings.

What is delightfully lacking from the Gemini environment is any serious indication of material pretension. The place and the pace are a little windswept, but Gemini is not too uptight about what gets blown away. Like a doughnut in a cyclone, everything will come around again.

What's your favorite restaurant anywhere? Why?

Tony Paco's in Toledo, Ohio. They singe their hot dog buns.

Was your mother a good cook?

Oh yes, everybody's mother is. She makes the best stuffed peppers. It's my favorite food. I once cancelled a date with Julio Iglesias, Wayne Rogers and Tom Selleck because she was serving it.

Gemini Favorites

Vegetable: asparagus, corn, carrots
Fruit: apples, oranges
Starch: potatoes, pasta
Source of protein: fish
Bread product: bagels
Dairy product: whipped cheese
   products
Spice or herb: pepper
Condiment: all; especially mustard,
   mayo, pickle relish
Ice cream flavor: vanilla, coffee
Pizza topping: olives and onions
Candy: M & M's
Cookie: bakery sugar

Sandwich: seafood salad on French
   bread
Soup: lentil with vegetables or broth
Soft drink: Diet Apple Slice
Beer: Amstel Light
Wine: sherry, aperitifs
Liquor: vodka
Liqueur: Kahlua, Midori
Comfort food: personal and plain
Celebration food: cake and ice
   cream
Junk food: corn chips, pizza
Sexy food: seafood, Italian

What's your favorite sandwich?

   I'm not a big eater. I don't like them.

   Italian hoagies.

What's your favorite cookie?

   Fortune cookies.

Gemini Diet and Health

Discussing diet and health with a Gemini is a little like talking to a ten-year-old about these subjects. There is some comprehension and belief, but there is a lot more boredom. Geminis would rather be outside playing.

Although their generally high metabolic rates and overall lack of primary concern with food tend to keep them on the lean side, Geminis can nevertheless be weight gainers. They tend to indulge in all variety of sensory gratification when they are mentally exhausted. And there are sometimes too many ill-considered snacks as opposed to well-balanced meals.

When a Gemini must diet, some authority/adult figure is frequently brought into the process. On the one hand, Geminis just won't easily swallow the generalized lore of any field of endeavor, invariably preferring personal investigation and consideration. On the other hand, someone playing the role of nutritional councilor or trainer introduces a role model for sincere and consistent behavior and, even more importantly for Gemini, establishes the opportunity for dialogue.

For the most part, though, the Gemini diet shows a marked preference for lighter foods such as fish, chicken, vegetables, fruit juices and complex carbohydrates. Ordinarily, of much more danger to Gemini than dietary abuses are the problems related to smoking. The Gemini is generally such an oral personality that a cigarette habit is most often a chain-smoking habit, and classical astrology has always associated Gemini with the functions and malfunctions of the lungs.

Fortunately, today most kids understand that smoking is a real no-no.

Do you ever diet?

Yes, but they are quick diets.

Do you have any personal nutritional beliefs or habits?

I think you should eat salads, but the stuff that's bad for you tastes better.

No, no, no, no, no.

Ten More Foods Most Geminis Like a Whole Lot

Chocolate éclairs • Italian subs • Pasta • Bananas • Cake
Cold cuts • Soda • Beer • Fruit juices • Olives

Things You Should Not Feed a Gemini

A lot of adult food when they are feeling like children
A lot of childish food when they are feeling like adults

Gemini Homefood

Geminis can't normally be troubled about what they are going to have for dinner. So much mind and mood changing goes on during the Gemini day that, from the perspective of 8 a.m., dinner-time might as well be in the next geological era. Grabbers and runners by nature, Gemini meals are made at the momentary impulse.

Of course, the traditional domestic forms of meal planning, shopping and cooking tend to waver from the average in such a life. Gemini kitchens are frequently barren, and household dining areas can be powerful testimonials to the profligacy of the take-out industry. An abundance of such items as wet-naps, pillow packets of ketchup and cartoon-festooned drinking glasses, along with the general buzz of Gemini energy, often conspire to give the impression that the Gemini household, particularly with regard to food, is a McDonald's.

Geminis possess the intelligence, but just don't usually possess the patience for most serious cooking processes. When they do cook it will be something that's quick and easy. Or else, on special occasions, it will be something that they themselves particularly enjoy, cheesecake for example, and they will have endeavored to learn an exceptional version.

When Geminis do take cooking seriously, they are particularly adept with knives and very much enjoy slicing and dicing ingredients for quick cooking in woks and sauté pans. When they entertain, Geminis will put out a lot of appetizers and finger foods so that everyone can walk around and talk while they eat. The food may not be filling, but it will be interesting and fun.

Where a Gemini will make the greatest concessions to domestic dietary responsibility is as a parent. Not only are Geminis smart enough to appreciate the importance of good nutrition in a child's physical development, they are fascinated by the mental development indicated through their children's evolving reaction to food and meal period socialization. Still, the child of the average Gemini parent had best develop a quick fondness for pizza and the Jolly Green Giant.

Was your mother a good cook?

She was okay. Consistent. She would always serve the same meals on the same days of the week. That was strange.

Approximately what percentage of meals do you eat away from home? Do you prefer eating out to eating at home?

100%, and yes.

Gemini Breakfast

In the early morning, Gemini has about as much enthusiasm for food as for toothpaste. They're both available and reasonable parts of the morning routine, but no big deal about the experience. Minimal application and effort—a little up and down and a cup of instant coffee—will generally do just fine.

Geminis never really like to have anything heavy in their stomachs drawing blood away from the brain, and this is particularly true in the morning. Not only do rich breakfast foods put them off as cranial clouders, but there's also deep aversion to projecting the freshly awakened consciousness into one's mouth. Geminis particularly reject the strong saline tastes and fatty textures of breakfast meats, and there's never much chance that they'll order steak & eggs.

Sometimes, on a holiday or weekend, the Gemini may go for a poached egg on a toasted muffin or a bagel & cream cheese. Deli-style omelets, like lox & onions or corned beef & Swiss cheese, are also occasional favorites, although these are most frequently ordered at lunch. Even on special mornings they will rarely prepare big breakfasts at home, as a Gemini can see no less appealing way to start the day than having to clean a kitchen.

Perhaps the time a Gemini really enjoys breakfast best is after having been up all night. This happens with some frequency, particularly during a Gemini's younger years, and is part of the reason why coffee shops and doughnut stores stay open twenty-four hours. But a Gemini eating breakfast after a sleepless night may, of course, actually be eating dinner.

It is hard to predict what they'll order, but it won't be steak & eggs.

Note 2: With Gemini, everything comes in pairs, including footnotes. The ampersand (&) was specifically invented for them, as they are the only creatures on earth who say "and" so often that they require an abbreviated form of the word.

What do you generally eat for breakfast?

Coffee and a bite of something fixed for the kids.

Who would be your choice of a fantasy companion for breakfast?

Anyone who would make it for me.

Gemini Breakfast Favorites

Juice: apple
Fruit: papaya
Cereal: Grape Nuts, instant hot oatmeal
Sweet roll: bear claws
Bread: bagels, muffins, croissants
Egg dish: poached on English muffins
Other: French toast with syrup assortment, coffee and tea

Gemini Awayfood

Geminis particularly love a warm greeting. Whether they're walking into a McDonald's, a neighborhood Chinese restaurant or ze finest restaurant in all of France, they simply want people to be happy they've arrived. This is largely because a Gemini is going to have a million questions and is hopeful of receiving patient and pleasant replies.

Ironically, the Gemini is the one who doesn't hear a thing the waiter says. The canned recitation will do for everyone else, but Geminis need personal explanations. What they're looking for is some friendly repartee, which is how they make themselves comfortable.

It's not just the restaurant manager and waiters who are expected to contribute to the dialogue. Dining companions and people at the next table are also expected to participate in animated and amusing banter. Hardly ever lazy and indulgent food affairs, Gemini meals are always times to talk.

Not unexpectedly, Geminis' favorite restaurants are casual spur-of-the-moment places. Fast food restaurants, diners and family chains get high marks for being omnipresent, cheap, informal and lively. They're also places where it's comfortable to read a book or newspaper if you're alone.

Dining out as often as they do leads Geminis into a certain amount of cuisine experimentation, and they develop affection for a fairly wide array of restaurant types. They are particularly fond of any savory bite-sized combination cuisines, and are invariably happy in Chinese restaurants, tapas bars and any place that offers a variety of toppings. For romance they are into seafood and Italian.

Although they are mentally eclectic—maybe *because* they are—one should not underestimate Geminis' ability to recognize superior restaurant performance. Their experience creates a wide spectrum for comparisons. They are not always sensitive to everything in the environment, but they can be astute about those factors, sensory and social, in which they are personally interested.

Geminis are also the people one frequently encounters at restaurant-sponsored wine tastings and cooking classes. They are lifelong learners and can find food as fertile a field for discovery as any other. Besides, they like it when local merchants go an extra step in catering to the needs, particularly the educational needs, of the community.

What is always truly likable about Geminis is that they will hardly ever play the snob, no matter what their level of accomplishment or expertise. They can turn temporarily weird and even throw the occasional tantrum, but they hardly ever err towards drenched sophistication. Dining with them can be charming and just a lot of fun, as well as mentally exhausting.

Oh well, if you can't keep up, you can always bring the waiter back for a spell.

What's important to you in the evaluation of a restaurant?

I like it when it's owner-operated. Then there is someone who really honestly cares that I'm there.

What's your favorite appetizer?

Escargots, if someone else is paying. Otherwise nachos.

I go right to soup.

What's your favorite entrée?

I prefer appetizers.

Romantic Menus for Gemini

To romance him:

Table: a stack of vintage comic books (preferably Classics Illustrated) or other clever reading matter
Appetizer: assorted vegetables, cheeses, crackers and dips
Salad: bibb with Caesar dressing
Entrée: chicken fajitas, with all the trimmings
Wine: Corona beer with lime wedges
Dessert: light cheesecake with fresh strawberry topping; coffee

To romance her:

Table: like to eat off coffee tables
Appetizer: relish tray with olives, pickles, mushrooms, artichoke hearts, vegetable relishes, etc.
Soup: won ton
Entrée: appetizer portions of: mussels marinara with spaghetti, escargots in garlic butter, sweetbreads in puff pastry, potato skins with exotic toppings
Wine: Wan Fu
Dessert: fruit-flavored ice cream and fortune cookies; tea

What's a romantic food?

Anything you can play with in your hands before putting it in your mouth.

Gemini Food Fantasy

A beautiful yacht is moored off the coast of Colorado. A brightly-colored party swarms merrily about the decks. The scene is framed by snow-capped mountains, and accented by native children vainly and comically attempting to throw snowballs at the yacht from the shore.

On board, Chinese food and bagels and lox are being served, in addition to a rather tempting paella. There is a complementary selection of wines and beer, and an assortment of light pastries that would make even Sara Lee weep for joy. Everyone is attempting, although not all are succeeding, to eat all of this food standing up.

In a cabin below decks, three lovers are enjoying the noisy party background in their afterglow. They are smoking cigarettes and saying the wittiest things to one another. A snowball flies through a porthole and they melt in giggles.

In the theater, a Gemini woman turns to a Gemini man.

"What's this movie supposed to be about?" she asks.

"It's about people who are having a party on a yacht off the coast of Colorado," he responds.

"Colorado doesn't have a coast," she answers.

"But it has snow and mountains," he counters.

"I guess you could say it has a coast," she concedes, "but not one with water next to it."

"Yeah, but it's a good party," he observes. "Just look at that paella."

"Ssshhh...," say several people in the seats nearby.

The Geminis smile guiltily at one another and simultaneously reach for handfuls of popcorn. The girl Gemini indicates her handbag in which a few beers have been smuggled into the theater. He nods enthusiastically and squeezes her hand.

"Was that a yes?" she wants to know.

"Yes."

Artichoke Heart Dip

submitted by Tom Frank

2 cans quartered artichoke hearts
1 cup mayo
1 cup grated parmesan cheese
1 t. garlic powder

Mix in soufflé dish. Bake at 350° for 1/2 hour. Serve with garlic toast.

Broccoli Salad

submitted by Lacy Green

1 bunch fresh broccoli
2/3 cup chopped green olives
1 small red onion, chopped
4 hard-cooked eggs, chopped
10 sliced fresh mushrooms

Dressing:
3/4 cup mayonnaise
1 T. lemon juice
1/2 t. sugar
salt and pepper to taste

Wash broccoli and dry well. Cut off florets, leaving 1" of stem. Dice remaining edible part of broccoli and add other ingredients. Mix dressing ingredients well and pour over salad. Toss and put in refrigerator at least 4 to 6 hours before serving.

Lobster Moosh

submitted by Linda Herzog

You take Velveeta, butter, and lobster and moosh it all together, then broil it on an English muffin. Talk about honesty!

Bread and Butter

submitted by Irena Chalmers

That's it.

Quick Chicken Hoisin

submitted by Kathy Matty

Chicken breast, boneless and skinned, cut into chunks
Hoisin sauce
Snow peas
Carrot sticks, celery sticks, red pepper, all cut in bite-size pieces
Cooked rice

Marinate chicken in hoisin sauce. Brown in wok or electric frying pan until almost done. Add fresh vegetables. Simmer until vegetables soften slightly (about 5 minutes). Serve over rice with fresh bread and Fuki plum wine. It's easy and it's colorful.

Birds of Paradise

submitted by Donna Lees

2 Cornish game hens
3/4 cup sliced scallions
4 cloves diced garlic
olive oil
pepper, dash
celery salt, dash
1/4 t. sage

1/4 t. thyme
1 large bay leaf
1/4 t. rosemary
1 cup chicken broth
1/2-3/4 cup sherry
1 cup mushrooms

In an electric skillet, sauté garlic in olive oil at about 250°, add hens and brown on each side, salt and pepper lightly. Add chicken broth, mushrooms, scallions, all seasonings and sherry. Baste hens with assimilated liquid, reduce to simmer and cook covered for 20-30 minutes. Serve with wild rice and fresh asparagus with hollandaise sauce (or something comparable). Serves two.

Cheese Cake

submitted by Annabelle Marquez

Filling:
3 8-oz. packages cream cheese
3/4 cup sugar
1 t. vanilla
3 eggs

Crust:
1 cup graham crackers
1/2 cup sugar
3 t. butter

Crust: Smash graham crackers into crumbs. Add sugar and melted butter. Combine thoroughly. Pour into spring pan and spread crust around the bottom of the pan. Pack firm.

Filling: Combine cream cheese, sugar and vanilla in a bowl. Blend until creamy. Add eggs one at a time. Pour on top of crust. Bake at 350° for 45 minutes or until you think it's done.

Italian Cheese Cake

submitted by Florence Paladino

1/2 cup candied diced fruit
1 cup milk
3 egg whites
3 egg yolks
1 whole egg

1 lb. ricotta cheese (15 oz. container)
1 T. sugar
2 T. flour
rind of one orange
butter and sugar (for cake pan)

Soak fruit in milk for 15-20 minutes. Heat oven to 375°. Butter and sugar an 8" soufflé pan. Beat the egg whites into a meringue. Mix all other ingredients together. Strain fruit (dispose of milk) and add to cheese mixture. Fold egg whites into cheese and fruit mixture. Bake in oven for 40-45 minutes.

Raspberries and Cream

submitted by Sandy Whye

Just so.

Hangover Soup

submitted by Gretchen Corral

Bring 2 cups of water to a boil. Drop in some bouillon cubes. Throw in cilantro and crushed chile. Let that boil for a little bit. When it's hot and boiling like crazy, drop in 2 whole eggs and let it get thready like egg-drop. And there goes your hangover. But don't go to the bathroom.

Some Gemini Food Personalities

Irena Chalmers, cookbook publisher, author and speaker
Elizabeth Alston, food editor, *Woman's Day*

Cancer

June 22 to July 21

Perhaps Anne would have liked a chance at having all the family's attention for those few hours. If so, she never got it. The stove, the bins, the cupboards, I had learned forever, make an inviolable throne room. From them I ruled; temporarily I controlled. I felt powerful, and I loved that feeling.

I am more modest now, but I still think that one of the pleasantest of all emotions is to know that I, I with my brain and my hands, have nourished my beloved few, that I have concocted a stew or a story, a rarity or a plain dish, to sustain them truly against the hungers of the world.

M.F.K. Fisher (Cancer), food philosopher
from *The Art of Eating*

I'd never work a job where they had a half-hour lunch.

Joanna Rose Light (Cancer), therapist

No one carries on a greater life-long love affair with cooking and food than a Cancer. Sure, kitchen work is occasionally a chore, and stomachs sometimes have a way of rebuking too much enthusiasm, but a Cancer is a born foodie. Right now, even as they read this, they are thinking about what to prepare and eat next.

Cancers are often given the knock for their moodiness, and the worst of their food habits are definitely related to their down times. They can balloon like the full moon when they are lonely or anxious. And they can also attempt to force food down the throats of others, especially their own young, if troubles are suspected.

To Cancers, though, the interconnectedness of food, family life and love is the foundation of their belief system. Providing food for one's brood is, to Cancers, the most spiritual, creative, powerful and loving act that a human being can perform. When it comes to an appreciation of food as sustenance—

spiritual, emotional, intellectual and biological—the subject's high priests and priestesses are Cancers.

Among the skills, besides an awareness that is rooted in the stomach, that a Cancer brings to this hefty responsibility are imagination, a practiced palate and a loyal memory. A Cancer is capable of much appetite-whetting creativity in meal planning, but there is never too much forsaking of the worthy past. Cancers do not abandon a delicious dish or a regular schedule of meal hours or frequent trips to the market just because the rest of society is into some sort of experimental fast-living phase—although they will occasionally admit new foods to their diet if these are *really* tasty.

Basically, a Cancer goes for "ordinary" foods: hamburgers, frankfurters, French fries, fried chicken, ice cream, bread, ribs, familiar international dishes, deli sandwiches, most ethnic home cooking. What they don't much care for is "ordinary" execution. A Cancer wants it done right—with exceptional flavor and texture, and some loving fussy respect in the plating and service.

This is true on all levels of the Cancer diet. They will eat fast food, but it will be at the place which has the most flavorful recipes and the most conscientious teenage cooks. In a fancy restaurant, they are usually happy to stick with the likes of shrimp cocktail and filet mignon, but there will be no second visit to the place that doesn't get these right.

To Cancer, the great culinary enemies are tastelessness and vapid trendiness. Cancers learn to distrust the enthusiasms of the in-crowd. Heaven remains lots of drawn butter on a lobster, or a sandwich at the Carnegie Deli, or the whole family sharing a good pizza.

And for tonight's dinner? Maybe a broiled shell steak that's been marinated in some teriyaki sauce, served with a baked potato and a glass of Burgundy. Start with a small salad with lots of tomatoes and crisp lettuce. Maybe get some vegetables and fried rice from the Chinese take-out place. And what about that garlic bread in the freezer? Hmmm, big meal, so maybe just fruit for dessert. And just a small slice of chocolate cake. With just a little ice cream on top. Hey, what's for a snack later?

In love—all night long.

What new trends in the restaurant scene don't you like?

I hate *nouvelle cuisine*, the pretension and the preciousness. Pictures on the plate. Small portions. I hate it. It's like the Emperor's New Clothes.

How preoccupied are you with the subjects of food and dining?

I think about what I'm going to have for dinner all day.

Ten Foods a Cancer Needs to Survive on a Deserted Island

Potatoes (all forms) • Beef (all forms) • Chicken • Seafood • Cheese
Tomatoes • Pasta • Bread and butter • Ice cream • Fresh fruit

What ten foods would you need to survive on a deserted island?

Coffee with milk; crispy, spicy fried chicken; sturgeon caviar on
toast; taboulah salad with a good amount of lemon and olive oil but
not too much parsley; babaganoush and warm pita bread; shell
steak; raw carrots, corn on the cob and asparagus; crispy, salty
french fries with tart dipping sauces; bean and cheese burritos with
tomatillo sauce, and cold, fresh water. Not necessarily in that order.

What ten foods would you need to survive on a deserted island?

I'm used to having everything.

Cancer Island

Each astrological sign is associated with a specific member of the solar
system. Cancer is said to be ruled by the Moon, and people born under this
sign are generally characterized as lovely, luminous, loony and of tidal emotions. "Moon-children," as Cancers are sometimes called, spend so much
time in their own ebbing and flowing interior emotional reality, that they
deeply require the nurturing and stabilizing influences of a family and a
secure home base.

In the real world, Cancers often settle best where there is a strong influence of the sign Cancer in a locale's horoscope. For example, both Oregon and
Washington became states at a moment with the Moon itself was passing
through the sign of Cancer. Likewise, the same astronomical event was taking place during the legal incorporations of the cities of Seattle, Spokane and
Salem.

In short, Cancer Island is more than vaguely reminiscent of the Pacific
Northwest. Cozy homes and neighborhoods, a temperate coastal climate with
plenty of moisture, a fairly unhectic lifestyle and an abundance of moonlit
forests are part of the desired mix. So is the fact that this is an area, to use

the phrase of a questionnaire respondent making a direct reference to Seattle, "where people give a damn about food."

Of course the Pacific Northwest has no monopoly in this last regard (interestingly, both New York City and San Francisco have strong Cancer placements in their horoscopes), but little can match this entire region's high regard for its own locally-produced foods and its own culinary traditions. Whether it is the Pike Street Market, Seattle's bountiful testament to regional food supply and cookery; or a coastal restaurant where a young chef dares to wed a local sweet berry to a local smoked fish; or simply a logger's home where the missus sneaks some molasses into the beef stew; there is an obvious pride, almost a sanctity, about what gets placed on a plate. Food in this environment nurtures both body and soul.

For all Cancers, wherever they actually live, a strong concern with dining is a basic essential of life. Somehow the notion of an "island kitchen" suffices. Which is where you'll find them when they're not with the Man in the Moon.

Do you like to cook?

Yes, very much so. I like the whole process of shopping and preparing. Going up and down food aisles is very stimulating to me.

Do you prefer eating out to eating at home?

Hell yes, I don't have to do the dishes. Seriously, cooking for only two is just no fun. I liked it better cooking for six when the family was growing up.

Cancer Favorites

Vegetable: cooked and seasoned
Fruit: pears, bananas
Starch: all
Source of protein: beef
Bread product: crusty and chewy
Dairy product: cheese, ice cream
Spice or herb: garlic, seasoned salt
Condiment: Tabasco, chutney
Ice cream flavor: caramel with nuts, coffee
Pizza topping: thick crust; double cheese, sauce, sausage, peppers and mushrooms
Candy chocolate—all varieties

Cookie: Mrs. Field's—all varieties
Sandwich: deli corned beef on sour rye
Soup: beef barley, lobster bisque
Soft drink: water
Beer: flavorful regional exotics
Wine: old Bordeaux, good Burgundies
Liquor: cognac
Liqueur: any served over ice cream
Comfort food: potatoes, pasta
Celebration food: anything delicious
Junk food: chips
Sexy food: seafood

What's your favorite vegetable?

I detest vegetables. I go many miles out of my way to avoid them.

What's your favorite fruit?

Bananas, especially in splits and milkshakes.

What's your favorite condiment?

The mustard on a Cleveland Stadium hot dog.

What's your favorite comfort food?

Spaghetti. I eat it a lot.

What do you generally have for lunch during the work week?

Aggravation.

Cancer Diet and Health

Here is an area where the average Cancer can use some compassion. They can't diet. They can't.

And what's more, they don't intend to.

What's the point of making it to a ripe old age, asks Cancer, if you're going to have to give up French fries, ice cream sodas, bakery goods and candy to get there? And life would be essentially meaningless without salt. And gee, now we're thirsty.

Cancers are prone to water retention, high blood pressure and all ailments of the stomach. They should use more discretion about what they eat? You might as well ask them to give up romantic longings.

They power eat when they are sad. They power eat when they are happy. When a Cancer is not hungry, it's time to call the ambulance.

Some Cancers stave off the inevitable in youth by becoming athletes or by pursuing some physically active line of work. Others are bulemics or are blessed with a few planetary placements in the adjacent high energy sign of Gemini or the adjacent vain sign of Leo. But in time a Cancer will almost inevitably lose the battle of the bulge.

Just don't bug them about it.

It's not nice and it won't do a bit of good.

Do you ever diet?

> Absolutely not. I've given up on the idea. I can't last a meal.

> It doesn't do a damn bit of good.

Do you have any personal nutritional beliefs?

> Not a one.

> No. I'm a firm believer that eating well means an absence of vitamin content.

> Stay away from fat and deep-fried foods unless it's calamari or really good French fries.

> I believe in consuming as much food you enjoy as you possibly can and still have the ability to cover the tennis court while fitting into last year's clothes.

Ten More Foods Most Cancers Like a Whole Lot

Jams and preserves • Cream cheese • Tuna salad • Oil and vinegar Coffee • Iceberg lettuce • Rice • Mayonnaise • Pickled herring Shrimp and lobster

Things You Should Not Feed a Cancer

Trendy food that doesn't taste good
Any bland food

Cancer Homefood

A Cancer's relationship to his or her own kitchen is almost too privately profound to be intruded upon with description. One could perhaps note the exceptionally fine collection of cookware and cutlery, the extra investment made in restaurant-grade ranges and refrigeration, or the compelling array of specialty food processing and cooking devices, all of which are likely to be discovered with above-average frequency in the Cancer kitchen. To concentrate on the externals, however, doesn't get near the heart of the matter.

The Cancer kitchen is, as M.F.K. Fisher has pointed out "a throne room." It is also a council chamber, a hermetic retreat, a wizard's workshop, a family gallery, a library, a psychiatrist's office, a safe harbor and a vault. To a Cancer, the place fairly glows with real powers, magical potentials and sacred commemorations, and there is little of importance in a human life that cannot transpire there.

A Cancer in charge of a kitchen feels like the master of fate. Menu planning and cooking, the Cancer knows better than any other astrological native, reflects and manipulates moods. A Cancer is the greatest of intuitive cooks.

Rarely does one see a Cancer consult a cookbook during the actual process of cooking. Part of the reason is that they have a good memory for recipes they've previously made, and their considerable culinary skills prevent them from straying too far from a proven path. The truth, though, is that Cancer will always change a recipe to suit the mood of the moment or the promptings of a well-stocked fridge, and even consider this intelligent spontaneity to be in large part what good cooking is all about.

Admittedly, Cancer does not always fare well in the baking department, where a sudden urge to experiment with egg and flour amounts is not necessarily going to yield improved results. Cancers are absolutely the best, though, when it comes to the virtuoso development of multi-dimensional stews and casseroles, which they will often make in humongous amounts and store in the freezer. Even with this stockpile, however, Cancers still love to compose simple spur-of-the-moment dishes like hamburgers, scrambled eggs and really terrific little English muffin pizzas.

Since Cancers' attitude about food seems to be present from birth, there is always a strong response to the food of their own childhood. If they grew up with mothers who couldn't cook or were otherwise oblivious to the sacred responsibility of mealtimes, there has yet to come forgiveness. Conversely, a mom who could bake bread and do a nice roast will be beatified in the memory.

Cancers will not make errors of culinary omission in their own homes, where there will always be too much food and too many encouragements to eat. The key is in understanding that Cancers use the ballast to prevent themselves and their loved ones from drifting away. They say "eat...eat," but they mean not to influence appetites but to capture emotions.

Do you like to cook? Why?

I love to cook. It's an achievement. You can be the worst cook in the world, and when you're finished you still have something to eat.

No. There was nobody to cook for but me.

Was your mother a good cook?

> The worst. She didn't enjoy cooking, she had to do it. I never liked her food. She burned things. Everything was greasy and ran together.

Cancer Breakfast

Think about a crab deeply buried in sand and you have some idea about a Cancer in bed. In either case, it would be hard to be more insulated from the affairs of the world. And it is definitely not easy to dig either out.

Food will sometimes work as a lure, but a Cancer can be a little particular in the morning. It's like a great musician tuning an instrument, the way a Cancer checks out the stomach for a while before composing the day's first meal. Often food will be forsaken for the first few hours of the day until mood, moment and menu converge just so.

Usually, though, a Cancer is ready for some serious eating by midmorning. This is not always practical, although a nine to five Cancer will come up with some rather ingenious methods for answering the call of brunch, often much to the amusement of co-workers who will swear there is a catering firm headquartered in the Cancer's desk. Cancer is very fond of the idea of brunch, as it allows for the consumption of breakfast or lunch foods, whichever sounds more delicious at the time.

Every once in awhile, a Cancer will get up quickly, go to the refrigerator, eat a few slices of last night's pizza and maybe drink a beer. Or you'll take them to an elaborate morning brunch and they will simply astound you with their enthusiasm for sampling every dish available—twice. This means they feel either very good or very bad.

They'll know when their stomachs tell them.

What do you generally eat for breakfast during the work week?

> I don't usually eat breakfast. My stomach doesn't wake up until about 10:30.

Who would be your ideal fantasy companion for breakfast?

> My friend's girlfriend. She's a baker.

Cancer Breakfast Favorites

Juice: freshly-squeezed citrus
Fruit: bananas
Cereal: pre-sweetened, with sliced bananas
Sweet rolls: coffee cake, pie
Bread: toasted English muffin with fruit preserves
Egg dish: pastrami and eggs with hash browns and sliced tomatoes
Others: deli bagel sandwiches

Cancer Awayfood

When a Cancer dines away from home, what matters is the food. This may sound extremely obvious, but there are plenty of other people who would put such factors as a restaurant's service, cleanliness, atmosphere and "crowd" on at least an equal footing with menu and kitchen performance. Not Cancer.

It's not that Moon-children are oblivious to the elements of the environment, but they are basically concerned with these to the extent that they aid or hinder digestion. Insofar as "contemporary" means stark décor, perfunctory service, loud entertainment, hectic energy and/or wantonly experimental/pretentious cuisine, Cancers are happy to be properly old-fashioned. They will gladly accept a little flocked wallpaper and a jukebox full of Sinatra if the kitchen knows something about flavoring food and plating generous portions.

In terms of "upscale" cuisine, Cancers are generally happy if a place can turn out a good steak, a scampi or a sautéed veal item. Do these well and serve them with a nice garden salad and plenty of starchy foods on the side, and a Cancer will be a customer for life. These people do not like to waste fine dining experiences trying the unfamiliar, and they will resist a lot of pressure to try a new spot about which they feel bad food vibes.

The same is true about neighborhood joints, many of which owe their long-term existence to the loyalty of Cancer patrons. Cancer will let someone else try such a place when it first opens. But the closing of a neighborhood restaurant that has been around for any appreciable length of time is as sad to Cancer as the loss of a good friend (although it will be a Cancer who reports that the food had been going downhill).

On any level of dining, Cancers simply expect that a restaurant will honor its own intentions and fulfill its own capabilities. They don't expect great Italian food from a pizza place, but they do expect a good pizza.

Finally, it is worth mentioning that a Cancer feels that romance should be conducted in restaurants but that serious business shouldn't. Food is almost exclusively a matter of pleasure and indulgence to Cancers. They want to put morsels of their dinner onto your plate and have you reciprocate by feeding them off your own.

This can be death during a job interview—but if it seems only naive, it's worth considering just how many Cancers own first-rate restaurants.

What's your favorite restaurant anywhere? Why?

The Carnegie Deli in New York. Because of the fact that when I bring a date there the sandwiches are too big and my date lets me finish hers.

What's important to you in the evaluation of a restaurant?

I like a place that understands its own capabilities.

How do you decide to try a restaurant you've never been to before?

Begrudgingly. I'm a creature of habit. Sometimes I'll take the recommendation of a very old and very trusted friend.

What new trends in the restaurant scene don't you like?

I'm glad *nouvelle cuisine* is on the way out. Paying $150 for dinner and then going to Burger King on my way home is not something I particularly enjoy.

Romantic Menus for Cancer

To romance him:

Table: fresh white linen; polished silverware
Appetizer: fresh shrimp cocktail with extra lemon, horseradish, Tabasco and oyster crackers on the side
Soup: lobster bisque
Bread: garlic French
Entrée: sautéed breaded veal cutlet; fresh tortellini with marinara sauce; steamed asparagus with drawn butter
Wine: white Burgundy
Dessert: fruit sherbert; heated cognac; if you can stand it, a good cigar

To romance her:

Table: the family photo album nearby
Appetizer: liver paté with chopped onion, egg, gherkins and cocktail pumpernickel
Salad: iceberg and garden vegetables, garlic croutons with dressing
Bread: oven-warm demi-loaf
Entrée: lobster tail with drawn butter; crispy French fries; corn on the cob
Wine: Chardonnay
Dessert: pear Belle Hélène; coffee

Who is your favorite companion for dinner?

Someone who says to me: "I'll eat anywhere, the movie is fine, your place or mine."

What's a romantic food?

Any food after the third date.

Cancer Food Fantasy

Cancer has a zillion tiny fantasies, and probably a half-zillion of them have to do with food. Moon-children belong to the realm of eating, body and soul. Their fantasies about manna are truly omnifarious and transcendent.

Let's grant the shy crab a little privacy in romance, although truly we are not just speaking of sensuality and affection here. There is a very reverential quality in the Cancer food fantasy. Cancer appreciates the relationship between sustenance and the Sustainer, and is not without a profound sense of gratitude.

Somewhere between romance and religion, though, is the average Cancer, who simply devotes a generous portion of life to the experiences and observations of eating. The food fantasy of such a person is to be in the company of beloved family and friends, to have available the talents and enthusiasms of a team of gifted chefs and ardent connoisseurs, and to get into some serious cooking, eating and talking about cooking and eating...

...all night long.

What would be your idea of the perfect meal?

Bad food with strangers. Then you wouldn't miss it.

Shrimp De Jonghe

submitted by Steve Stone

For two, definitely.

1-1/2 lbs. large shrimp, painstakingly peeled and deveined, which is the worst part.

Sauté this in as much butter as you have in the house.

Combine garlic powder, garlic salt and fresh chopped garlic in an amount depending on whether you are married or single. Married people can have more garlic because their spouse can't leave.

Add garlic to taste.

Add Italian-seasoned bread crumbs.

Add some more garlic.

Dump everything into aluminum foil; seal and place in a 325° oven for 10 minutes tops, 5 if you're hungry.

Take it out and go get 'em.

Chicken Curry

submitted by Stan Cook

Don't measure. This is done by feel. Brown pieces of chicken in butter and oil. Add any inexpensive wine (you're going to butcher it with spices) so that there's enough for sauce. Add cut-up cauliflower, broccoli, onions, potatoes, carrots and any other firm vegetables. Add bananas, prunes, 2 to 3 large tablespoons of jelly or jam, lots and lots of curry powder, extra cumin and turmeric, African paprika and cayenne pepper. Add soft vegetables like zucchini or any other squash. Simmer down until thick. Serve with rice, fresh succulent fruit like papaya, plain yogurt, chutney and any innocuous fresh bread.

Smoked Salmon Fettucine

submitted by Mark Caraluzzi

1 lb. spinach or regular fettucine
1/4 lb. unsalted butter
2 t. garlic, finely chopped
2 t. shallots, finely chopped
24 oz. heavy whipping cream
1 T. Dijon mustard
1 t. salt

1 t. black pepper
3/4 lb. smoked salmon (Nova Scotia style is best), thinly sliced
1-1/2 cups freshly grated parmigiano cheese
1/2 cup fresh chives, finely chopped
8 lemon wedges for garnish

In a skillet large enough to hold all the ingredients, melt the butter and lightly sauté the garlic and shallots without browning for 4 minutes. Cut 3/4 of the total salmon amount into strips and leave the rest in large pieces for garnish. With the heat on low, add the cream, mustard, salt and pepper and mix all the ingredients well. Bring to a simmer, cut heat and set aside until needed. Cook pasta, drain well and add to the sauce with the parmigiano cheese. Bring to simmer while tossing. Immediately portion out into warm serving bowls and garnish each bowl with the large pieces of salmon, the fresh chives and two lemon wedges. Serves four.

Spaghetti alla Carbonara

submitted by Priscilla Cockerell

1 lb. spaghetti, cooked *al dente*
3 strips bacon, cut into 1/2-inch pieces
1/3 cup white wine
3 eggs
2/3 cup freshly grated parmesan

Fry bacon until done, but not too crisp. Drain some fat. Pour in wine to deglaze; cook and reduce a little. Pour this mixture over pasta and toss. Whisk eggs and cheese together; pour over pasta and toss.

Kugel

submitted by Joanne Rose Light

8 oz. package of flat egg noodles
8 oz. cottage cheese
8 oz. sour cream
1 T. honey
1/2 cup raisins
cinnamon

Heat oven to 350°. Cook noodles and drain. Blend together the cottage cheese, sour cream and honey. Add the noodles and stir. Add the raisins and cinnamon to taste. Pour into a buttered casserole dish and bake approximately 30 minutes or until light brown on top. Cut into squares and serve.

Schmaltz

submitted by Shirley Freedman

Put chicken fat (and cleaned chicken skin if you wish) into sauce pan. Add a *lot* of chopped onions. Do not add any water. Cook at low heat until onions turn brown. Strain into glass container. Keep refrigerated. It will last for several weeks. You can use chicken fat on any beef to add a slightly different taste. Try brushing on to steaks or barbecue shortly before serving—it's luscious.

Some Cancer Food Personalities

Wolfgang Puck, owner and chef, Spago and Chinois restaurants, Hollywood and Santa Monica, California
Ted Balistreri, owner, The Sardine Factory restaurant, Monterey, California; past president of the National Restaurant Association
Ferdinand Metz, president of the Culinary Institute of America

Leo

July 22 to August 21

---

*I was hooked. In love with it all. With the human contact,
the smells and the tastes. The sensuality. The affection
and the tension, the noodles and the waitresses, the pantry and the pantry girl, the customers and the waitresses,
the food and the waitresses. I loved the camaraderie, and
the things we did. I loved the people. And while I never
married a waitress, or got any deeper in the noodle dough,
I've never fallen out of love with the humanity, the
warmth, the social person-to-person feeling of the restaurant business.*

Joseph H. Baum (Leo), restaurateur

*Food is never an issue of survival. It's an issue of pleasure
and sharing, of human connection. Some of the happiest
moments of life come sitting around a dining room table.*

Ann Yonkers (Leo), foodie

Leos tend to act as if they are starring in plays about their own lives. While
this theatrical self-centeredness can become wearisome to the supporting
players, there is still a lot in a Leo to admire. In any situation, no one has a
greater instinctual capacity than a Leo about how to mine a moment's glory.

Leos experience life as tragicomedy, and are capable of great extremes of
happiness and sadness, courage and cowardice, success and failure. The
greatest measure of experiential quality to a Leo—whether one speaks of
achievements, relationships, possessions or dining experiences—is the indication of an involved heart. For better or worse, Leos live by instincts and
feelings far more than they do by judgment and intellect (which in a Leo is
rarely weak, and is often quite creative, but must be led by the senses and
affections).

When it comes to their food lives, and so much else, it is impossible to
ignore the symbolism of the cat. Leos literally enjoy many of the same foods
as felines, especially dairy products, fresh fish, foods that are aromaticized

with garlic and onions, and fresh water. (Ironically, several Leos asked about their favorite cookie or cracker responded "goldfish.") Much like the finicky Morris, Leos are very sensitive to a food's full range of sensory components—and will flat out reject that which does not appeal to all the senses, while heartily embracing anything/all that does.

It is not merely the substance of the Leo diet, but the style that invokes the feline. Leos particularly love to wander, or be coaxed, into unknown and unique dining situations, and to be generously fed, stroked and otherwise entertained. Anyone who satisfies these desires is considered by the Leo to be a friend—or at the very least a loyal subject.

Leos' tendency towards regality should not be confused with snobbery, as there is nothing that Leos dislike so much. They are more partial to energy than form and, while enjoying most elegant environments, are happy to be served nachos, pizza, spaghetti, French fries, ice cream, or cheeseburgers; anything but the tortured ambiguities of a practitioner *de cuisine*. In general, a Leo disdains the dryness of petty detail (where the chef got his training, which of the flowers on the plate is edible), endeavoring instead to support personal enthusiasm, generosity of spirit and honest achievement wherever they may be encountered.

Above all, Leos enjoy the social aspects of dining. Whether it's a chorus of caterwauling or an intertwined tale for two, Leos prefer to arrive at table in company and will often decline to dine if they must do so alone. Consider the cat, or the king, who will eat nothing that does not first pass by someone else's palate.

Most often, though, a Leo has an enthusiastic appetite for food and life in general. A Leo on a diet is generally a Leo with a heartache. Food is not a matter of the intellect or even an issue of survival to the Leo, but an area of human connection and petting concern.

Is your mother a good cook?

She really isn't. She only cooks because she has to. It's her job. But her heart isn't in it.

What's a romantic food?

All food is romantic.

Ten Foods a Leo Needs to Survive on a Deserted Island

Pasta • Wine • Cheese • Mexican food • Garlic and onions
Milk and cream • Eggs • Bread • Tomatoes • Fruit basket

Pick a holiday in which food plays an important part. Name it and briefly describe the food.

Leo birthdays are so important. Birthday cake and champagne.

What's the most interesting thing in your refrigerator?

A $60 bottle of champagne that a man I met in a disco brought to me.

Leo Island

In the Leo environment a happy balance is struck between the need for personal space and the desire for social contact. The cat covets a comfortable, perhaps somewhat opulent, private retreat, but does not wish to be too far removed from the action. Fond of reflective solitude, the Leo also wants some source of friendly stimulation and attention to be pretty close at hand.

While Leos are traditionally associated with thrones and satin pillows, some more modern manifestations of their desires are large town homes, dramatic lofts, garden patios and crystal-clear swimming pools. Leos like to inhabit theatrical, generally bright and open spaces where they can entertain and hold court, and the kitchen/dining areas of many a Leo residence give evidence of this. Of course, what makes the Leo style work is the availability of a large and dutiful service force, and the maids, gardeners, pool attendants and caterers on Leo Island considerably outnumber the Leos.

At heart a party animal, the Leo requires access to a lively municipal center, be it modelled on Manhattan or cloned from a beach community on the California coast. The Leo goes for the throb and sensory stimulation of nightlife. Restaurants and clubs on Leo Island are the conceptions of stage-crafters, with crowd, cuisine, lighting, musical accompaniment, etc. all being orchestrated into a polished performance of background pizzazz.

You may not actually see the Leos swagger or strut into these establishments, but that is only because you are not inside their minds. Leos simply love to be the focus of attention. These are the people who actually appreciate the enthusiastic ministrations of disc jockeys, strolling violinists, cigar cutters and mariachi bands.

Even the more family-oriented trade on Leo Island is comprised of establishments that are heavy on the hoopla. Diner re-creations, pizza restaurants with pipe organs, specialty delis run like carnivals, the average McDonald's, are all in evidence here.

Happiest, though, is the Leo being wined and dined at one of the many romantic seafood restaurants along the island's shoreline. Here is where one may witness a Leo's most engaging performances. Just don't forget to applaud.

Do you like to cook?

Yes, because it fulfills a creative desire. Every time I cook it's a dramatic performance.

What do you generally eat for lunch?

I have to eat lunch or I get run down. When I was young and sexy, I skipped it.

Leo Favorites

Vegetable: green beans, zucchini
Fruit: oranges, pineapple, banana
Starch: potatoes, pasta
Source of protein: fish
Bread product: onion rolls, whole grain
Dairy product: milk
Spice or herb: pepper, tarragon
Condiment: salsa
Ice cream flavor: coffee
Pizza topping: loaded, especially extra cheese
Candy: caramels

Cookie: butterscotch chip
Sandwich: tuna melt with tomato
Soup: Yankee bean
Soft drink: coffee
Beer: idiosyncratic favorite
Wine: Chardonnay
Liquor: vodka
Liqueur: Amaretto
Comfort food: milk and cookies
Celebration food: champagne
Junk food: Fritos, Goldfish
Sexy food: white chocolate mousse

What's your favorite fruit?

Starfruit.

What's your favorite liquor?

Chivas Regal.

How do you like your pizza?

With lots of stuff. I like lots of stuff on my stuff.

Leo Diet and Health

To face the matter squarely, the Leo is ordinarily a vain creature. Dietary appeals to this sign are not best made by nutritional counselors. The Leo has far more respect for the opinion of a mirror.

It's not that the Leo chooses to be contrary in the face of scientific evidence. As a group, Leos tend to restrict red meat intake, eat a lot of fresh fruit and vegetables, limit cholesterol, and augment vitamin and mineral deficiencies with supplements. They do this, though, mainly to look and feel attractive—the dryness of the scientific debate on the subject of nutrition, not to mention any act of self-denial, leaves them quite cold (and most Leos hate being cold).

One will generally find a Leo ready to rout a few nutritional negatives for the sake of a good time. The expression "eat, drink and be merry..." is far more Leonine than "a penny saved...." Subsequently, loved ones will do well in advising their Leos to be "heart-smart," which is exceedingly appropriate on a personal level.

When they do diet, Leos generally have to make a fierce and conscientious commitment to the process. They are disposed towards dietary aids (Leos love to feel their blood race) and to rigidly-structured calorie reduction programs that promise all the pleasure of complete meals with none of the pain of abstinence. But no one has really developed a complaint-free diet as far as the Leo is concerned.

Quite often, a Leo on a diet is suffering from some romantic disappointment. But when enough pounds have been shed in sorrow, and the Leo puts on some Danskins and returns to the aerobics studio—well, the grin on that new lean body, and the admiring stares it garners from others, are enough to make the Cheshire cat seem a sourpuss.

Do you ever diet? How?

Yes. I used to eat Figurines. I loved 'em. I really got off on 'em. They were delicious.

I try sometimes after a binge or a vacation. I decrease my caloric intake from 3,500 to 3,000 calories a day—just kidding.

Do you have any nutritional habits or beliefs?

I know there are lots of things I shouldn't eat that I eat all the time.

Ten More Foods Most Leos Like a Whole Lot

Fresh fish • Peanut butter • Water • Vodka • Beer
French fries • Crackers • Cookies • Ice cream • Bakery desserts

Things You Should Not Feed a Leo

Licorice
Sour/pickled foods

What are some foods or flavors that turn you off?

Any really fishy-tasting fish, especially sardines. I think I like everything else.

Leo Homefood

If it's true that real hospitality must come from the heart, then the Leo is truly the great host of the zodiac. Oh, details may escape them and social crises be inexpertly covered up, but no one extends a more sincere welcome to a guest. It often seems that Leos live to entertain and to be entertained by others.

Where Leos run into trouble is that they're not the sort of people to pay scrupulous attention to the contents of the cupboard or to pay excessive heed to the physical and temporal laws of cooking. Leos will charmingly persuade you to join them at home for supper, and then suffer surprise equal to your own upon learning that the refrigerator contains nothing but mold, a box of baking soda and a year-old fruit cake. Even so, they may be tempted to whip something up from these ingredients (Leos revel in being creative), but they will then often poorly estimate the limits of patience and taste appeal.

Here it's probably worth mentioning that Leos expect to be flattered—for their cooking no less than in other regards. Even when they are good cooks, however, they are not to be counted upon to cook *often*. Leos like to cook when *they* are hungry, otherwise they are happiest when someone else is handling the chore—although they will want to give advice and encouragement to the chef. (To Leos, a cherished culinary compliment is being told they selected the right caterer for a party.)

One important exception to all of the above is in the category of coffee. Leos generally adore coffee—as a flavor, as a source of water enhancement, as a receptive medium for milk products, as a stimulant to get their hearts racing, and as an acknowledged elixir of the *tête à tête* and *klatsch*. Their kitchens and cupboards usually give ample evidence of this preoccupation with brewed beverages, and any Leo invitation to come over for a cup of java should be accepted as a sincere compliment.

Just remember to bring some Danish or something, if you're counting on eating.

Do you like to cook?

Yes, but I like it better if someone cooks for me.

Was your mother a good cook?

Not particularly. But she was a wonderful entertainer—she put that in my heart.

Do you prefer eating out to eating at home?

It depends on who's coming and who's cooking.

Leo Breakfast

Leos, whose planetary emblem is the sun, are usually fond of mornings. The desire to rise and shine comes naturally to them. So does, on the other hand, a certain amount of tanning attitude, and it is almost certainly a Leo who coined the term "beauty sleep."

When they do rise early, Leos are more likely to be breakfast eaters than skippers. They love the foods of morning (dairy products, breads and cereal grains, coffee, orange juice), which they eat because of enthusiasm for their tastes, not nutritional considerations. No one is more gastronomically stimulated or guilt-free than a Leo attacking a well-prepared order of Eggs Benedict, especially when served with a nice big lapping bowl of café au lait.

Leos can always abide affectionate company, but they are as equally pleased to have some solitude in the morning. Glamour often takes time to get together, and Leo doesn't want to reveal every bit of stagecraft that goes into rôle preparation. Also, Leos try to remain pretty well-informed about current events—especially as they relate to leading personalities—and enjoy having some time to look at the morning paper.

In quite a few Leo hearts is the fantasy of a breakfast attended by a cast of characters such as: the president of the United States; the premier of Russia; the Pope; the ghosts of Winston Churchill, Walt Disney and Casey Stengel;

several powerful international business magnates; an equal number of glamorous, sensitive and intelligent movie stars; and, of course, the Leo. Over some thickly-buttered bran muffins and exceptional coffee, this group would confront and cure any and all ills confronting the planet. And, best of all, no one would have to actually *do* anything, because everyone would have their own large and competent staff of Virgos to handle the details.

What do you generally eat for breakfast?

I like mornings, I wish my body would. When I'm up, I eat a lot.

What do you have if you're enjoying a special breakfast?

I love all bakery stuff—bran muffins, good croissants, cinnamon rolls. I'd be happy forever with just bread and fruit. And coffee—don't forget coffee.

Leo Breakfast Favorites

Juices: orange, pineapple, apple
Fruits: tropical fruit salad
Cereal: flakes with bananas and milk
Sweet roll: fruit and bran muffins
Bread: variety toast and variety jams
Egg dish: poached eggs, specialty sausages, hash browns
Other: Eggs Benedict; café au lait

Leo Awayfood

Leos do not like restaurants in which the food has to be explained to be appreciated. Such food demands too much attention, argues the Leo, who is very sensitive about appearing ill-informed. Also, the average Leo doesn't much care to share the spotlight with anything that eventually passes through an intestine.

This is not to imply that the Leo is without a sense of adventure when it comes to restaurants. Few people are more willing to try a new place on a recommendation, a hunch or just because they're hungry and find themselves in front of some place to eat. Leos love pleasant surprises—they just don't care for explanations.

Neither should it be assumed that the Leo has a boring palate. The lion loves the spiciness and good times flair of cuisines like Mexican, Italian and Chinese. The Leo just does not covet the esoteric for its own sake—items such as nachos, lasagna and egg rolls are favorites because they are good, and most ethnic restaurants can be counted upon to turn out decent versions of items such as these.

Not surprisingly, a Leo is quite put off by the recent appearance on the restaurant scene of the celebrity-chef phenomenon. Leos sincerely feel that cooks should be in love with preparing and serving food, not with themselves. And besides, if everyone in the restaurant is paying attention to the chef-presence, who is going to admire the Leo-presence?

In terms of service, a Leo is a great deal more pained by pretentiousness than familiarity, although the astute service person will not press the latter too far. Leos like it when people catch the warmth of their personal glow, but they're not crazy about sharing the limelight. They can be strong sticklers for common etiquette when it comes to the manners of service personnel.

Whatever else a restaurant offers in terms of food, service and atmosphere, it must woo the Leo by creating an opportunity for the guest or customer to star. Leos are happiest in restaurants with dramatic lighting, reflective surfaces, bright music, multi-level seating (to see and to be seen), high-back booths and anything else that establishes flattering background. They particularly love celebrations in such circumstances, with plenty of dancing, singing, chatting, drinking, fond testimonials, gifts and awards.

What's really unexpected, given this scenario, is that Leos more often than not prefer to eat at home. In their own lairs they simply have more control over establishing environment and selecting the crowd. Sometimes, though, they just can't find someone else who's willing to do the cooking and cleaning up.

Do you prefer eating out to eating at home?

I love to go out, but it loses its novelty if you do it all the time.

How do you decide to try a restaurant you've never been to before?

Word-of-mouth, or I'm driven in by a severe and debilitating hunger. I've found some gems that way.

What new trends in the restaurant scene don't you like?

I hate *nouvelle cuisine*—the whole hustle.

What turns you off in restaurants?

I hate waiters, especially pretentious French waiters. The French are so ill-suited to be waiters.

What's important to you in the evaluation of a restaurant?

Service, quality of food, who I'm with. I can put up with a lot sometimes if I'm enjoying the company.

What's your favorite restaurant anywhere? Why?

There was a place in Chicago where I fell in love with someone. The
food was pretty good too.

Romantic Menus for Leos

To romance him:

Reception: Lillet with orange slices; honey-roast nuts
Appetizer: melon and prosciutto with breadsticks
Soup: vichysoisse
Entrée: rare grilled tuna with orange beurre blanc; julienne carrots and
     zucchini; French fried potatoes with ketchup
Wine: Riesling Kabinett
Dessert: hot apple pie with coffee ice cream and butterscotch; Remy Martin
     and French cigarettes

To romance her:

Table: as much sparkle as possible; background melodic jazz
Reception: champagne cocktails and Chinese egg rolls
Salad: leaf lettuce with mild onions, exotic mushrooms, garlic croutons and
     raspberry vinaigrette
Entrée: salmon en croute; new potatoes; green beans polonaise
Wine: Pouilly-fuisse
Dessert: Pot de Crème; selection of liqueurs and coffees

Leo Food Fantasy

It is a cliché to most, but not to the Leo heart—a sunset veranda overlooking
a storybook beach, happy sad melodies in the background, fine wines and
sweet ocean fish, a few exceptionally good friends and, most important,
someone special to adore the Leo. And if everything clicks just right—a
perfect cup of coffee.

Leos like fantasies that make them laugh.

What would be your idea of the perfect meal? What would you have served? Who would you be with? Where would it take place?

Any and all of the above.

One of each.

Ooooo....

Sweetbread and Wild Mushroom Salad

submitted by John Jackson

sweetbreads

wild mushrooms

garlic

shallots

soy sauce

oyster sauce

cornstarch

salad greens

Flour sweetbreads in cornstarch. Heat sesame oil in wok. Cook sweetbreads until almost done. Add wild mushrooms, garlic, shallots, soy sauce and oyster sauce. Take out of wok and place on a medley of greens including arrugala, radicchio, red leaf, Boston and watercress. Serve with raspberry vinaigrette dressing.

Peasant Soup

submitted by Jan Mactier

6 leeks, chopped into bite-size pieces
6 potatoes, chopped into bite-size pieces
1 T. salt
1 cup cream

Place vegetables and salt in soup pot. Cover with water and simmer for 20 minutes. Turn off fire and add the cream. Voilà!

Onion Soup

submitted by Kevin Leonard

5 cups thinly-sliced onions
6 T. butter
1 quart stock or water
1 T. tamari
3 T. dry white wine
1/2 t. dry mustard

a dash of thyme
a few dashes of white pepper
salt to taste (1-2 t.)
Optional:
2 small cloves garlic, crushed
1 t. honey

Cook onions and garlic, lightly salted, in the butter in a kettle. Cook them until very-but-not-too brown. Use medium heat to cook them gradually and thoroughly. Add mustard and thyme. Mix well. Add remaining ingredients. Cook slowly, covered, at least 30 minutes.

Pineapple Dressing

submitted by Carol Fry

1/2 cup butter
1 cup sugar
4 eggs

1 can crushed pineapple (1 lb. 4 oz.)
5 slices bread, cubed

Cream the butter and sugar. Add the eggs, one at a time. Fold in the crushed pineapple, and the bread cubes. Bake in greased casserole at 350F for 1 hour.

Peanut Butter and Jelly Sandwich

submitted by Richard Atcheson

butter
peanut butter
jelly
2 slices bread

Butter the bread slices, then apply first peanut butter, then jelly, as required. Serve open-faced.

Five Mushroom Pasta

submitted by Bunny Martin

1/3 lb. each, any kind of exotic mushrooms (shiitake, cloud's ear, morels, chanterelles, angel wing)
1/3 to 1/2 cup butter with fresh-chopped summer savory
1-3/4 cups cream
salt
pepper

Sauté mushrooms in butter and savory. Add cream and simmer until reduced and thickened. Add salt and pepper. Toss with 8 oz. fresh hot pasta. Serves about four.

Barbecued Pork Tenderloin

submitted by Jane Kirby

1/3 cup honey
1/4 cup soy sauce
1/4 cup olive oil
juice of 2 limes
2-inch piece fresh ginger, peeled and minced
2 garlic cloves, minced
1 jalapeño pepper, seeded and minced
2 T. fresh thyme or 2 t. dried thyme leaves
2 pork tenderloins (3/4 lb. each)

In a small bowl combine honey and remaining ingredients except tenderloins. Place tenderloins in a heavy plastic bag. Pour marinade over pork. Seal bag. Refrigerate at least 4 hours. Cook over medium hot coals about 10 minutes, turning to brown on all sides. Slice and serve. Makes 4 servings.

Note: Do not overcook or pork will be stringy and dry. Tenderloin may be served slightly pink in the center. This works well on swordfish, too.

Tofu Scrambler

submitted by Cynthia Joyce Iliff

It's made by Fantastic Foods. Quick and easy, three steps. For further instructions, read back of box!

Apple Cake

submitted by Wendy Ring

1-1/4 cups oil
1-1/2 cups sugar
3 eggs
3 cups flour
4 cups peeled and diced apples

1 cup chopped nuts
1 cup raisins
1 t. vanilla
1 t. each—salt, baking soda,
   cinnamon

Stir oil and sugar in with eggs and vanilla. Sift dry ingredients and combine with batter. Add remaining ingredients. Pour into greased and floured 9" tube pan or two small loaf pans. Bake at 350° for 1 hour. Cool in pan.

Seven-Layer Cookies

submitted by Brenda Black

1 cube butter, melted
1 cup graham cracker crumbs
1 6-oz. package chocolate chips
1 cup shredded coconut

1 6 oz. package butterscotch chips
1 cup chopped walnuts
1 can Eagle condensed milk

Put the first six ingredients in a 9" x 12" baking dish. Cover with the condensed milk. Bake 30 minutes at 350° degrees.

Some Leo Food Personalities

Julia Child, TV personality, cookbook author
Joseph H. Baum, renowned restaurateur and consultant
Jane Kirby, food editor, *Glamour* magazine
Susan Sarao, food editor, *Seventeen* magazine
Jean Hewitt, cookbook author, food editor, *Family Circle* magazine

Virgo

August 22 to September 21

He does not go to restaurants, and the reasons are several. They make a fuss, and the owner or cook's on his neck like a gnat. Or worse, it's a stream of sports fans (still Ted's worst epithet) with napkins to sign. At restaurants you wait, wait, wait. Restaurants have little chairs and tables, no place for elbows, arms, knees, feet. At restaurants there's never enough food. Lastly, restaurants charge a lot, and Ted doesn't toss money around.

The last reason is seized upon unkindly by restaurateurs in Islamorada and nearby Keys: "No, he doesn't come in. He's too cheap. He'd go all over town, sonofabitch, and he'd pay by check, hoping they wouldn't cash the check, they'd put it on the wall."

But this is resentment speaking, and it is Ted's lot in life to be misunderstood.

Richard Ben Cramer, on Ted Williams (Virgo), in "What Do You Think of Ted Williams Now?"

Do Virgos eat any junk food?

Leona Fitzgerald (Virgo), cooking instructor

A Virgo's life is a serious confrontation between the rational mind and the myriad requirements of everyday living. The mind hopes to make some sense of life's vast input, to observe correctly and order priorities, and to prompt the total human organism into reasonable and appropriate action. This is, of course, a lot easier said than done.

Life has some good laughs at the Virgo's expense, primarily because the Virgo is so earnest about life. About getting all the details right. About making sense. About making dollars. About everything.

Virgos generally believe that life should be lived according to sober ethical and moral principles: everything in moderation; give more than your best and expect less than your due; idle hands are the devil's tools. Of course no one, not even a Virgo, can live up to these tenets all the time. And while they themselves do their best to act with purity, the Virgo ends up thinking of most human behavior, including their own, as flawed.

Blessed (cursed?) with an amazingly sharp intellect and powers of observation, Virgos cannot help but notice the speck of turbulence in a sea of calm. Lacking the foolishness and faith of the artist, they practice the discipline and dogmatism of the critic. In the professional food world, they comprise a significant percentage of food editors, restaurant reviewers and dietitians.

Virgos are tremendously stimulated by the vast amount of precise detail in food-related subjects: the encyclopedic possibilities of comparative grocery pricing; the tortuous teaspoon tabulations of complicated recipes; the milligram gospel of nutrition. They love fussing with the complexities of menu planning and entertaining, and more than anything they love critiquing factors which don't measure up. Their assessments rarely overflow with warmth or kindness, but they are always practical and precise.

Virgos know a lot of facts about food, although again theirs is the insight of the skilled commentator rather than the artist or sensualist. Virgos are not entirely without inspiration or strong appetite, but they are not very comfortable with extreme flights of fancy or indulgence. They're the sort of people who take just a few bites of everything on the plate, making notes all the while, and who'll then ask for a small taste of everyone else's dessert.

Since they are generally moderate and self-controlled, it is extremely interesting to observe a Virgo who has fallen prey to some culinary compulsion and who must wrestle with the devil's food as a result. Actually, chocolate is a particularly vicious temptation to Virgo, and there are many troubled "chocoholics" in Virgo ranks. Virgos hate their own weaknesses and will go to extravagant lengths to conquer them (dieting Virgos are the ones who tape heart attack graphs and photos of naked fat people to the refrigerator).

Eventually a Virgo gets the humor of the human predicament or is crippled under its weight. Whatever the outcome though, there is definitely something ennobling in the quest of the Virgo who envisions a world where everything lives up to its potential.

If only everything could be like, like—tuna fish! This Virgo favorite has so many virtues. It's good in fancy recipes or plain out of the can, it's familiar, it's non-fattening (unless you bury it in mayonnaise), it's nutritious, it's inexpensive, it's kid-pleasing, it's portion-packed, it's probably even in the cupboard—it's enough already.

What's your favorite restaurant anywhere? Why?

It was on a lake in an old house. There were small rooms, it was quiet, classical music played in the dining rooms. The food and service were excellent but there was no pressure. It burned down.

Ten Foods a Virgo Needs to Survive on a Deserted Island

Bread • Chicken • Water • Wine • Fruits and vegetables
Chocolate • Butter • Potatoes • Ice cream • Cheese

Virgo Island

Everybody thinks they work too hard. Except Virgos. They're too busy working to give it much thought.

Virgo Island is the home of the earnest laborer, to whom skill, diligence and service are the greatest goods. The place is reminiscent of a colonial or frontier town where the blacksmith, barkeep, parson, porter, clerk, deputy, schoolmarm, herdsman, doctor, farmer, et al. are always to be found in their appropriate environments, earnestly participating in the life of the community while making a buck for themselves.

The key to a Virgo paradise is "a place for everything and everything in its place." Their environments are often a tenuous balance between a finite amount of space and the zillion useful things which may be crammed into it. Virgos simply want all possible resources close at hand, as nothing more frustrates them than reaching out for a tool, or a fact, that is not immediately available to be pressed into service.

The Virgo shopping environment is typified by thick eclectic shop-by-phone catalogues and sprawling discount warehouse stores. Sales are popular. So is home delivery.

Catering, both social and institutional, is also much in evidence here. As a customer, Virgo expects a professional approach to the logistics of mass feeding situations. As caterers themselves, Virgo are at their best handling the details of a big buffet.

As for the Island's food establishments in general, there is a pleasant lack of pretentiousness or plastic. Virgos generally crave the simple, pure and natural, and would ordinarily rather eat a salad or some frozen yogurt in a health food store than patronize the glittering (and expensive) palaces of gourmandism. There is evident fondness for little peasant-cuisine establishments, particularly Mexican, where Virgos can celebrate the sensibly-priced gustatory glory of foods such as chips, salsa and refried beans.

Somehow, though, stores selling expensive imported chocolate, rich bakery fare and fine wines also manage to stay in business.

On Virgo Island, everyone stays in business.

What's your favorite restaurant anywhere? Why?

I don't like to eat at my favorite restaurant too often. The food is too rich.

Virgo Favorites

Vegetable: salad ingredients, crudités
Fruit: tree, tropical
Starch: baked potatoes
Source of protein: chicken
Bread product: garlic French, whole wheat
Dairy product: cheese
Spice or herb: garlic, seasoned salt
Condiment: mustard
Ice cream flavor: chocolate almond
Pizza topping: everything except anchovies
Candy: almond chocolate

Cookie: brownies
Sandwich: chicken or tuna salad on whole wheat
Soup: lentil
Soft drink: soda
Beer: Mexican with lime
Wine: Chardonnay
Liquor: vodka
Liqueurs: Frangelica, Cognac
Comfort foods: chocolate, potatoes
Celebration food: caviar
Junk food: popcorn
Sexy food: pasta with cheesy cream sauces

What's your favorite candy?

Chocolate. Hershey's chocolate. There's nothing like being specific. I also have M & M's in the freezer.

What's your favorite source of protein?

Tofu. But it's not a complete protein.

What's your favorite alcoholic beverage?

Crème de cassis and Perrier. Cassis has more vitamin C than orange juice.

What's your favorite celebration food?

You have to have dinner first.

Virgo Diet and Health

Virgos are mightily concerned with daily living, and so they are naturally involved with the subjects of diet and health. No one is more "up" on nutrition, nor is anyone so readily disposed towards the effort of disciplined exercise as a Virgo. Temperance, clean living, hard work and the basic food groups are all a Virgo really needs in this lifetime.

That and a lot of water, because the Virgo is the purification addict of the zodiac.

It was likely a Virgo who decided that human beings should (could!) drink eight large glasses of water a day. It is also the Virgo demanding "no additives and nothing artificial" of America's food industry. Virgos are the sort of people who consider popcorn a junk food.

While this may seem finicky to others, most Virgos have simply made an honest attempt to study (often with copious notes) the impact of ingestion on their own systems. Sometimes even real food produces undesirable reactions in Virgo. They are not, therefore, eager to mess around with the likes of chemical preservatives.

It is ironic, considering the preceding, that Virgos seem prone to more dietary maladies and adverse food reactions than natives of other signs. It is conceivable that they manage to train their systems to be especially intolerant of impurities and chemical imbalances. It is also likely that these incredibly busy people don't always have the time to practice what they preach—perfection is so demanding.

Perhaps the real key, though, is that many Virgos are just plain compulsive about eating. Not only is food a certifiable necessity of life, there's just so much about it to catalogue and critique and simply to enjoy. And what the heck—with enough iced tea you can flush out anything.

Do you ever diet? How?

Yes, it's the story of my life. Poorly.

About once a day I talk about it.

I try. It's a very depressing subject. I think I'm hooked on sugar.

Do you have any personal nutritional beliefs?

Yeah. I'm a real elimination fanatic.

Ten More Foods Most Virgos Like a Whole Lot

Soft drinks • Milk • Beer • Coffee • Tomatoes
Beef • Popcorn • Lentils • Shrimp • Tuna fish

Things You Should Not Feed a Virgo

Intensely sugary foods
Artificial flavorings and colorings

Virgo Homefood

Virgos have the most completely stocked larders in the universe (Cancers sometimes have more food, but no one has greater variety than Virgo). We're not just talking staples here, although there are always ample amounts of those. Rare is the Virgo fridge that doesn't contain the likes of Thai bean paste or marinated brussels sprouts, or the Virgo pantry without a full range of curry garnishes or an entire line of imported beverage mixes.

Their equipment cabinets are also treasure troves of culinary catholicism. A Virgo's private gadget and serviceware collection can put most kitchen specialty stores to shame. There is also usually enough tupperware and other storage material to seal the Titanic.

One readily assumes from such factors that Virgos love to cook and to entertain, and they usually do, but they don't very often. Cooking, especially when one is congenitally incapable of a haphazard or spontaneous performance, simply demands too much time and effort. Good scout Virgo is prepared for anything, but more often than not reaches for the microwave at mealtime.

When the Virgo does cook it is frequently a superb performance, although a Virgo is more than ready to point out any shortcomings in the results. They'd usually much rather plan a meal—coordinate the menu, shop for the ingredients, select the serviceware and table appointments, place the guests, create the mood, etc.—than actually cook it. Virgos can be quite compulsive when it comes to scrupulously following recipes, but they are not especially gifted in visualizing outcomes or adjusting to special sets of cooking circumstances (and so they'll cook tried and true favorites again and again).

Virgos are scathingly straightforward in their critical appraisal of other cooks, including their own mothers. If there is an idealized family cook it tends to be a grandmother who labored under more primitive conditions and therefore had to expend a good deal more diligent effort in getting meals to come out right.

What did grandma cook that was particularly good?

Everything, but...

What's the most interesting thing in your refrigerator?

There's so many interesting things I can't begin to tell you.

What is there more of than anything else in your refrigerator?

Peanut butter. I got a good price so I bought extras.

What's your favorite kitchen gadget?

I have some kitchen shears from Zurich that I use for a lot of things. I used them to cut up carpet for the bathroom.

Was your mother a good cook?

My mother was a good cook but she didn't like to. My mother said that her mother was so excellent a cook that she couldn't live up to her. I inherited my mother's sense of disappointment.

Virgo Breakfast

Conceptually, breakfast may well be the Virgo's favorite meal. All that grain and fruit for purification and all those complex carbohydrates for energy. And there's even a morning newspaper serving up a fresh batch of mindfood.

Nevertheless, it is often the case that the presence of a Virgo, who is frequently the detail person at a place of employment, is essential to the start of the business day. Add to this that a Virgo has a tendency to feel five minutes late for everything and you end up with someone who frequently forgoes a morning meal. True, breakfast doesn't have to be an indulgence, but when Virgos set their minds to something, details have a way of bloating into day-long distractions.

So the Virgo generally skips breakfast—to deny a craving is a perversely pleasurable duty—and occasionally makes up for it with an elaborate Sunday brunch. This last can take the form of a buffet blitz, a deli demolition or an omelet orgy. The only essential ingredient is the company of a mate, friends and/or family. Sadly, busy Virgos never seem to have quite enough time for the important people in their lives and a big Sunday breakfast is a form of atonement—and a great excuse for some serious chowing down.

What's your favorite meal?

Breakfast seems better than other meals. I don't really know why. At dinner you can be disappointed. Not so much at breakfast.

Who are your favorite lunch companions?

Good friends who are bad influences.

Virgo Breakfast Favorites

Juices: orange, apple
Fruits: fresh tropical fruit mix
Cereals: Nutri-Grain, Shredded Wheat
Sweet rolls: bran muffins
Bread: whole wheat toast
Egg dish: variety omelets with fried potatoes
Other: fruit and yogurt

Virgo Awayfood

Virgos cannot ignore details, and when they dine out they notice everything. Are they greeted courteously upon arrival? Are they seated promptly at the precise time of the reservation? Is the table properly set, the floor clean and the air free of off-odors?

And so it goes, right up until the valet parker receives his meager gratuity, smiling nonetheless, and gently but firmly closes Virgo's door.

Likewise during the actual meal itself, Virgos do not so much eat as check out the performance of the kitchen. They tend towards ordering small portions of many different foods which they then chew slowly, evaluating the effect of each flavor in the dish, of each dish in the meal and of each meal on the menu. Virgos are very fond of combination entrées, tapas assortments, wine and cheese buffets, people who'll share off their plates—any dining situation catering towards the Virgo desire for *complementary diversity*.

Taking into consideration that Virgos like to talk and share information, that they are generally more relaxed in company than when they are alone and that they just plain like to eat, one might expect Virgos to be happy in most public dining situations. The truth, though, is that anyone who looks as hard for imperfections as a Virgo is eventually bound to find one, and a flaw can gnaw away at a Virgo like a flea on a dog. When the imperfection is uncovered, as it frequently is, in the areas of service or pricing, Virgo irritation can seem a lot more like anger.

Regarding prices, the Virgo just knows too much about specific ingredient costs to accept fully the mark-ups that restaurants charge for food. Oh, they're aware that labor, rent, electricity and so forth must figure in, but they are not happy when the hamburger here costs two dollars more than the same-weight hamburger there and all that's been added to the plate is a pickle. A Virgo's frugality is based upon sound information, but it is frugality nonetheless.

Even an outrageous price does not, though, raise a Virgo's ire as much as does bad service. The zodiac's sign of devotion and purity, Virgos understand to the depth of their being that service is a function of the right skill and the right information, coupled with the right behavior at the right moment. A restaurant service person who is unfamiliar with the menu, ill-groomed, inattentive, obtrusive beyond the point of helpfulness or too concerned about a tip is an abomination to Virgo.

All Virgos are restaurant critics—some are just smart enough to get paid for it.

What's important to you in the evaluation of a restaurant?

> The most important thing is the knowledge of the waiters and the waitresses. If they don't know anything about what they're selling me, I'm p—d off. If I owned a restaurant, service would be my number one concern.

What turns you off in a restaurant?

> I'm so opinionated, nothing just simply turns me on or off. I hate it when a restaurant blatantly tries to put something over on you, like charging prices that are plainly arrogant considering the mediocrity of the food. I'm not stupid.

Romantic Menus for Virgo

To romance him:

Small portions!
Table: matching utensils (appropriate to each course)
Appetizer: escargot in puff pastry with garlic butter
Salad: tossed wild greens with light vinaigrette and homemade croutons
Soup: seafood bisque

Entrée: prime rib; potatoes Anna; tri-color fresh vegetable timbale
Wine: a good Cabernet Sauvignon
Dessert: chocolate truffles and Cognac

To romance her:

Smaller portions!
Table: coordinated and spotless
Appetizer: beluga caviar purses
Salad: chopped, with cheese, tomatoes and poultry
Entrée: grilled swordfish with olive salsa; polenta; roasted peppers
Wine: Chardonnay
Dessert: white chocolate mousse with bittersweet chocolate sauce;
      frangelica and coffee

What's a romantic food?

Anything in cream sauce except chipped beef.

Virgo Food Fantasy

Since Virgos usually place rather strict conditions on their actual behavior, they very often compensate with wonderfully rich fantasy lives. In private, the Virgo is truly among the sexiest of the signs. In their dreams, they're also among the most bulemic.

It's only when they talk out loud about their fantasies that the restraint and qualification inevitably creeps in. Suddenly the fantasy wine must have a very specific label. Then the fantasy croutons must be homemade and tossed with, not added to, the salad, which may have arrugals but not bibb. And let's have some carefully selected friends who are known to share, and we'll order small portions, and we'll all meet exactly at eight o'clock....

Virgos really do crave abandonment but they are stalled by the sharp edges of reality and responsibility. They dream of love, but they believe in imperfection. Joy is so remote.

And yet, sometimes, just the right tuna salad in just the right fantasy....

Who would be your ideal fantasy companion for lunch?

A cat of some sort.

Spicy Korean Barbecued Ribs

submitted by Jane Snow

2-1/2 lbs. pork spare ribs
1 cup soy sauce
1/4 cup sugar
1-1/2 t. fresh minced ginger
2 T. minced garlic

1/4 cup vegetable oil
1/2 cup sliced green onions,
  including tops
2 T. lemon juice
1 T. crushed red pepper flakes

Trim ribs of fat. Cut slab into individual ribs. Combine remaining ingredients in deep bowl and mix well. Submerge ribs in marinade, cover and refrigerate four hours.

Prepare charcoal fire. Sear ribs on both sides, two inches above coals, for 2 minutes a side. Raise grill to 4 inches above coals and cook until done, 20 to 30 minutes. Serves four.

Chicken Enchiladas

submitted by Judy Viskocil

1 cooked and cubed chicken breast
1 can cream of chicken soup
1 can diced green chiles
1 t. chopped onion

1 cup sour cream
1-1/2 cups grated cheddar cheese
1/4 cup milk, approximately
10 corn tortillas (fast fried to soften)

Mix first five ingredients and about 1 cup of cheddar cheese. Spoon about 1 T. of mixture into tortilla and roll. After all tortillas are filled add milk to mixture and pour over tortillas. Top with remaining cheese and bake for about 20 minutes at 325°.

Shrimp and Spinach Purses

submitted by Peter Finkhauser

Filling
3/4 lb. shrimp (peeled and coarsely
    chopped)
5 oz. spinach
2 t. flour
1-1/2 T. butter
2 oz. fish stock
1/3 cup onions; minced
2 T. scallions; minced
salt, to taste
black pepper, to taste
cayenne, to taste
nutmeg, to taste
Pernod, to taste
1 t. garlic

Dough for purses:
3 t. sugar
3 t. butter
1/4 t. salt
1/4 t. cayenne
2 eggs
1/4 cup milk
2-1/2 cups flour

Filling: rinse spinach well, cook in salted boiling water until tender (about 5 minutes). Drain very well and chop medium coarse. Sauté onions in butter until soft. Add shrimp, garlic and scallions. Sauté for 1 minute; add flour and cook for 2 minutes. Add stock and smooth out with whisk. Add spinach and blend well. Season with salt, cayenne, nutmeg, black pepper and pernod. Enough filling for about six purses

Dough: cream together sugar, butter, salt and cayenne. Beat eggs with milk. Blend butter mixture, milk and eggs, and flour.

Assembling purses: on a floured board, roll out dough very thin. Cut into 6" circles—make six circles. Distribute filling among them in the center of each circle. Wrap dough around filling, forming a bulb shape. Crimp dough tightly at the top to seal the purse. The neck of the purse should be as thin as possible to insure even cooking. Deep fry (375°) until golden brown; bake for 5 more minutes in 375° oven.

Grilled Tofu Steaks with Tropical Salsa

submitted by Leona Fitzgerald

3 lbs. firm tofu
Marinade:
2/3 cup vegetable stock
1/3 cup safflower oil
1/4 cup lemon juice or white wine
1 T. red chile flakes
2 bunches cilantro, washed and
 finely chopped
1/4 cup minced fresh ginger
freshly ground pepper
15 cloves garlic, smashed (peels
 removed)

Pineapple or Mango Salsa:
3 mangos, very ripe (about 1-1/4
 lbs.) or 1 large pineapple
3 T. chopped cilantro
1/2 jalapeño chile, minced (or more,
 to taste)
a pinch of pepper

Combine marinade ingredients in large baking dish. Drain water from tofu and cut each piece lengthwise into 1" steaks. You will have twelve total. Place on towels and allow to dry for 30 minutes. Add tofu to marinade at room temperature for 2-3 hours.

Meanwhile, make salsa. Peel mango or pineapple and coarsely chop fruit. Transfer to bowl and add remaining salsa ingredients. Set at room temperature for 1 hour before using.

Preheat grill or broiler. Oil or spray grills or broiler pan with Pam. Place tofu steaks on grill and cook for 4 minutes on each side, basting constantly. Serve with a side of salsa and a dollop on top of steaks. Garnish with cilantro and avocado slices.

Oysters Scampi

submitted by Iris Chapman

highly seasoned bread crumbs
whole oysters
3 cloves of garlic
lots of melted butter

Shake oysters in plastic bag with bread crumbs. Press garlic cloves into melted butter. Spread oysters in flat pan, pour garlic butter liberally over all and broil until just bubbly and crumbs begin to brown.

Killer Cornbread Stuffing

submitted by Judy Hille

6 T. butter
3 onions, chopped coarsely
1 cup celery, chopped
8 cloves garlic, chopped
2 4-oz. cans chopped green chiles
2 boxes Jiffy cornbread mix,
    prepared according to package
    directions
1 t. sage

3 t. cumin
2 red bell peppers, diced
2 lengths spicy sage-flavored
    sausage meat
2 eggs, beaten
a generous shake of cayenne pepper,
    or 4 small dried hot chiles
4 cups chicken broth

Cut or break cornbread into small pieces and crumbs. Spread on cookie sheet and dry. Stick in oven overnight, or bake in slow (250-300°) oven 45 minutes or so.

Sauté in 4 T. butter, the onion, garlic, green chiles, cumin and sage until lightly browned. Set aside. Fry sausage and red bell pepper, breaking sausage up with fork and frying until lightly browned. Drain grease, if any.

Toss onion mixture and sausage mixture with cornbread, adding the small dried red chiles and the beaten egg. Spoon into greased 4-quart baking dish, pour chicken broth over, and bake at 350° for about 1/2 hour, covered, then return to oven uncovered for another 10 or 15 minutes.

Chicken and Rice

submitted by Cheryl Jackman

1 chicken
Crisco
1 can of tomato soup
small can of tomato sauce
2 large onions

salt
pepper
paprika
garlic powder
rice for four servings

In a large pot brown onions in Crisco. When beginning to brown add liberally-seasoned chicken. Mix sauce and soup and add to pot. Bring to a boil. Reduce heat and simmer for 1-1/2 hours. Divide chicken and serve in sauce over cooked rice.

How-Now Brownies

submitted by Sue Zelickson

1 (12-oz.) package chocolate chips
3/4 c unsalted butter or margarine
4 eggs
3/4 cup sugar
1 t. vanilla
3/4 cup whole wheat flour

Heat oven to 350°. Melt chocolate and butter together in microwave or over medium heat. Stir and let cool slightly. Beat eggs by hand in large bowl; add sugar and vanilla; continue to beat until smooth, 2-3 minutes. Add chocolate mixture and flour; stir well. Pour into greased 9" x 13" cake pan. Bake for 20-25 minutes. Cool; cut into squares.

Tomato Salad

submitted by Lisa Ekus

I don't want to give you a real recipe, but rather something I love to make almost every night during the summer when the produce is fresh and readily available.

Combine fresh tomatoes (cut into chunks), fresh cucumbers (optional), scallions and lots of finely minced garlic (must be fresh also). Add fresh basil (optional). Season with fresh pepper to taste. Drizzle with olive oil and the vinegar of your choice. Toss and enjoy.

Some Virgo Food Personalities

Craig Claiborne, food editor, *New York Times*
Betsy Balsley, food editor, *Los Angeles Times*
Jane Snow, syndicated food columnist, *Akron Beacon Journal*
Judy Hille, food editor, *Arizona Republic*
Jim Nassikas, president, Stanford Court
Spiros Zakas, noted restaurant designer

Libra

September 22 to October 22

Oreilly stayed with her in the room over the weekend. It was like the most beautiful party Sylvia could remember; she'd never laughed so much, for one thing, and no one, certainly no one in her family, had ever made her feel so loved. Oreilly was a fine cook, and he fixed delicious dishes on the little electric stove; once he scooped snow off the windowsill and made sherbert flavored with straw-berry syrup. By Sunday she was strong enough to dance.

Truman Capote (Libra), author
from "Master Misery"

I'd say that food is the third most important thing in my life. First is family and friends and their good health. Sec-ond, I really can't think of anything but I feel I should leave a blank. Then comes food.

*   It really is a big part of my life because my husband is in the restaurant business and it is important to him.*

Donna Chase (Libra), interior designer

Everything is in harmony and humming along smoothly. Suddenly, an op-posing force enters the picture. It will be a Libra who first notices.

Libras are challenged by anything that disturbs the natural flow of their perception. This may mean strongly-discordant sense impressions or any unexpected disruptions of a reasonable course of events. It can come with inner inspiration or simply be the sudden awareness of someone else's awareness.

A Libra's primary urge is to be the equal and opposite force that balances all other forces. This makes Libras fundamentally reactive, but it does not make them passive. Strong-spirited people, Libras have definite ideas about the way things should and should not be.

We should be fair and honest with one another, reasons the Libra. We should avoid the ugly and the evil, and pursue the beautiful and the good. We should be sane and live in peace.

And in the process, we should not take a lot of crap.

Libras can be very impatient about crap. They are sincerely offended when someone mucks up their world with a gross performance and they have to make a response. They will not willingly have their attention called to poor taste or shoddy workmanship, disliking pretentiousness (a crime of self-importance) and bad craftsmanship (a waste of money, effort and time) in equal measure.

When it comes to culinary matters, the Libra can definitely be one tough cookie to please. Food and dining are always significant matters to a Libra. Even beyond personal needs and tastes, the Libra values dining as a realm of social ritual, as a practical commercial enterprise, as a field of aesthetics and as an activity of love.

Libras are the avowed enemies of mindless menus and inhospitable dining environments. They can easily live without funky food combinations, frozen vegetables and bad attitudes in service personnel. They also won't eat much stuff like liver or cabbage, unless it has been prepared by someone they love—a lot.

When it comes to their daily care and feeding, Libras expect consideration rather than excess. They like well-produced versions of simple foods far more than novelty for novelty's sake. If they are involved with fine foods and wines they will certainly appreciate being served some, but they are not unreasonable when it comes to confining these to "special occasions." The moderate menu they would take to survive on a deserted island is considerably different from the fare of festivity or fantasy.

As adaptive and reactive people, Libras are just not long on food fanaticism, although they will soundly reject the bad and support the good. Their real intention is to make human interaction a little more palatable, and that generally gets down to the golden rule. They are willing to try the pizza someone else's way.

It is to the everlasting credit of Libras that they most often pursue peace and partnership as life's greatest goods. To the Libra, cooperation is a beautiful chord of simple harmony amidst an endless cacophony of struggling cross-purposes. A delicate touch, modesty and sweet sincerity are qualities that a Libra brings to any table.

Thank goodness someone does.

How do you know you're in a good restaurant?

I like it when there's a statement on the menu about having patience because they are preparing your food.

What would be your idea of a perfect meal?

A barbecue sandwich with Lee Trevino between holes on a great golf course.

Ten Foods a Libra Needs to Survive on a Deserted Island

Chicken • Eggs • Water • Potatoes • Bread
Milk • Cheese • Oranges • Premium protein • Peas and carrots

What's the most interesting thing in your refrigerator?

There's nothing terribly interesting in the refrigerator.

Libra Island

At first sight, the island of the Libras seems unremarkable. Nothing in the environment demands attention. Everything is peaceful.

A second look confirms that it's a genuinely lovely place with a subtle sense of charmed reality. Crank up your perception and something mildly sweet drifts in on a breeze—new-age flute or juniper pine. There is an easy harmony of natural and man-made detail.

It is not a flashy place but one whose human society is eminently respectful of its environment. Homes are comfortable parts of a hospitable landscape, and are built with patios, picture windows and large, airy rooms. There are many easily-accessible parks, ponds and picnic spots hosting an amiable amalgam of recreation, repose and romance.

The islanders' favorite restaurants are built along the lines of the homes. Inside and out they are considerate of the environment, featuring simple, beautiful food and unobtrusively skillful service. Nothing is hurried or loud in these establishments, their primary tone being that of natural intimacy.

Things move at a somewhat faster clip in downtown Libra City, where the island's inhabitants work, shop and occasionally take in a show. Here, food service establishments run the gamut from neat little dives (Libras are not snobs, and know good price/value when they see it) through popular singles bars (Libras are flirtatious and romance has to start somewhere) to the finest of French restaurants (also romantic, and Libras will gladly patronize quality when they can). There are plenty of casual mom and pop places, too, where the food is basic and good and the owners are still in love with one another.

Perhaps unexpectedly, the Libras do their grocery shopping at a huge modern supermarket. While they have a liking for the sort of food sold in specialty stores and delicatessens, they prefer the time-saving ease and convenience of having everything under one roof. Sometimes, they simply love drifting up and down the regularly spaced aisles with their shopping carts, seeing if anything catches their interest and smiling at strangers.

What new trends on the restaurant scene don't you like?

I don't like places that are too chic—edible flowers and everything served on a croissant.

Libra Favorites (It depends on what *you're* having.)

Vegetable: asparagus (or peas)
Fruit: strawberries (or apples)
Starch: pasta (or potatoes)
Source of protein: beef (or chicken)
Bread product: sourdough (or bagels)
Dairy product: cheese (all kinds)
Spice or herb: pepper (or garlic)
Condiment: mustard (or mayonnaise)
Ice cream flavor: nut fudge (or butter pecan)
Pizza topping: onions, mushrooms, pepperoni and olives
Candy: peanut butter cups (or chocolate caramels)
Cookie: oven-warm chocolate chip
Sandwich: grilled cheese and fresh tomato on bakery bread (or cheese-
   burger—or chicken salad)
Soup: potato-leek (or vegetable beef)
Soft drink: water (or coffee)
Beer: regional favorite (or premium import)
Wine: premium dry white (or premium dry red)
Liquor: vodka (or Scotch)
Liqueur: unpredictable, but knowledgeable
Comfort food: soup (or ice cream)
Celebration food: fancy dessert (or a delicious dessert)
Junk food: cheese-flavored chips (or potato chips)
Sexy food: lobster (or chocolate mousse)

What's your favorite pizza topping?

Pepperoni. And they never give you enough to cover the whole pie.

I used to like plain, but my wife introduced me to olives and onions. Now I love it that way.

What's your favorite candy?

Mon Chéri chocolates.

What's a romantic food?

Salad. Do I have to explain why?

Libra Diet and Health

Libras are moderate by nature, so they do not often need to make dietary prohibitions the central concern of life. To pay some attention to the basic food groups, limit fats and sweets, and, if they gain weight, to restrict caloric intake, is about as much nutritional credo as Libras can take. Even this is pursued in a fairly unconscious fashion as Libras are not the sort willfully to overdo much of anything.

OK, everybody knows one or two overweight Libras. Hey, they're human. It can happen.

Most Libras will simply start skipping some meals if they feel the need to lose weight, no big deal. There are those Libras, however, who really appreciate the dynamics of group support and prefer to pursue such programs as Weight Watchers. The Libra enjoys attending the meetings with a good friend, which enhances the sincerity of the commitment and provides someone to laugh with in private about the broader characteristics of the group.

If moderation is a built-in practice, it is also a strong Libra principal to avoid too many beliefs that restrict the opportunity for variety in personal experience and response. A Libra enthusiastically enjoys an occasional slice of roast beef, an order of super nachos or a to-die-for chocolate dessert, and resents the attitude of the people who proclaim such foods inherently bad for health. One Libra questioned about dietary beliefs had recently forsaken vegetarianism and proudly proclaimed herself "a born-again carnivore."

Willingness to change behavior plus a subtle touch of humorous self-effacement is a large part of the Libra charm. When it comes to the lack of desire to eat everything in sight, they're just lucky.

Do you have any nutritional beliefs?

No. I wish I did.

I enjoy what I eat, but I won't over-eat. Just because something is good, I don't feel I have to take seconds.

Ten More Foods Most Libras Like a Whole Lot

Ground beef • Nuts • Shrimp • Tomatoes • Coffee
Cookies • Pasta • Wine • Mushrooms • Ice cream

Things You Should Not Feed a Libra

Overly pretentious, faddish foods (e.g. pan-blackened *nouvelle cuisine*)
Anything that tastes or smells a lot like boiled cabbage

What are some foods or flavors that turn you off?

Liver. I'd rather eat a sneaker. And anchovies—yuck.

Libra Homefood

Few signs feel more strongly than a Libra that life is about what happens after you leave home. A young Libra is so eager to escape the nest because "out there" is where you get to meet everybody else. There's just no personal latitude in selecting parents or siblings.

"Out there" one can also get knocked around quite a bit, Libras especially, as they have that innate need to remain responsive and even-keeled. This is why one aspect of a Libra's home life takes precedence over all others. For a Libra, the home is a refuge where one can comfortably put up one's feet and periodically visit a calm and unguarded personal reality.

As anyone who has ever cohabitated with a Libra can attest, their most common home pose is: seated in a favorite chair (often a rocker); reading, listening to music, or watching TV; perhaps munching on some cheese or chips while sipping a beer or a glass of wine. There is an air of dreamy depletion about them at such times. Ask a question and the response will be close to inaudible, if there is any acknowledgment at all.

The Libra is truly absent at such moments, much like the car when it is in the shop. It will generally run fine when you get it back, but it is fruitless to hurry the process. The nicest thing you can do for Libras at these times is to go into the kitchen and make them some cookies or a chicken salad sandwich.

When the Libra is feeling a bit more vibrant there is a willingness to accomplish a fair share of the household chores, including an occasional turn in the kitchen. The Libra usually prepares simple meals of few courses, but they are stylish and good-tasting nonetheless. The exception to this pattern is the preparation of special romantic meals, at which the Libra naturally excels, and where all sorts of lovely food and libation are possible.

For the most part, though, a Libra at home is a Libra at rest. It's OK if things get a little crazy in the kitchen around Thanksgiving and Christmas. But that's enough.

Do you like to cook?

I like to go into a kitchen, whip up a storm and leave. I don't like to clean up. So I guess I probably have a knack for it, but I don't pursue it.

No, because the people around me want a whole meal and I only like to cook one dish at a time. And my husband won't let me use the "S" word—Stouffer's.

Was your mother a good cook?

It seems like she was at times but, in reality, no, she wasn't. But I'll kill you if you tell her.

Libra Breakfast

One of the deep, dark secrets of too-good-to-be-true Libras is that they are sometimes just a trifle grouchy in the morning. Not even a Libra wakes up with a desire to take people's abuse all day. They need a little time to prepare themselves.

As for food, the average Libra requires little more than coffee for breakfast, although simple carbohydrates are often consumed for the additional energy boost. A Libra can sometimes be seduced by a fast food breakfast sandwich, which has certain subtle virtues of taste and nutrition and can be easily purchased and consumed. A total turn-off is lead-heavy cold leftovers from last night's dinner.

Although Libras appreciate some space in the morning, they are avid radio listeners and newspaper readers. The average Libra would particularly enjoy having as a breakfast guest someone like Paul Harvey or Phil Donahue, people with strong viewpoints about the popular-interest issues of the day. Most Libras wouldn't want these people dropping around all the time, however, as they seem to need a heck of a lot of attention.

Libras enjoy a well-prepared omelet late on Sunday morning, particularly if prepared by an affectionate mate. But they are also capable of preparing their own omelet and pretending that they're sharing it with some beautiful companion. The Libra may have some trouble deciding on what to put in the omelet under the latter circumstances, but is happy in the knowledge that there won't be any trouble over who gets first crack at the funnies.

What do you generally eat for breakfast during the work week?

Not much.

What do you have if you're going to enjoy a special breakfast?

I don't like large breakfasts.

Libra Breakfast Favorites

Juices: orange, apple
Fruits: melon, strawberries
Cereals: oatmeal with brown sugar, butter and milk; granola
Sweet rolls: wheat and nut muffins
Bread: bagels with cream cheese
Egg dish: bacon, cheese and mushroom fritata with salsa
Other: banana pancakes with macadamia and coconut syrup

Libra Awayfood

A Libra is always ready to support any enterprise based on demonstrable sincerity regarding the public welfare. The effort can be moral, mental, economic, aesthetic, physical or spiritual, or any combination thereof, and can be made in any endeavor of mankind. The Libra always admires true *greatness*, when individuals enlarge themselves by increasing the quality of life or easing the burden for others.

Suffice it to say if a Libra designates a restaurant, be it temple of gastronomy, mom and pop diner or taco stand, as a "favorite," you can be pretty confident it's a special caring place. Libra finds it a necessity to eat out often, and are themselves very solicitous of sincere recommendations and favorable critical reviews. They assume there is a reason when a place becomes an in-spot, although they will certainly reserve judgment until it is experienced firsthand.

What scores points with a Libra will be any food prepared in a manner that reflects workmanship, integrity and taste, the way the Libra would cook if there were enough time. They expect intimacy, comfort and congeniality in the environment. Libras need to relax and it is important that any dining experience is simply *pleasant.*

Libras are turned off by dining experiences that feature too many surprises or go to jarring extremes. They don't like secret molten centers in microwaved foods or fruit sauce on their steak. They avoid harsh lighting and loud features in the environment, and the extremes of obsequious familiarity and overblown formality in service.

When it comes to actual menu selections, Libras are interested in, but not blind followers of, fashion. Their favorites are often popular classics like cheeseburgers, shrimp, French onion soup, steak, lobster and chocolate desserts. They like their pasta with meatballs and tomato sauce, and their Chinese food with rice and fortune cookies.

Remember, though, that the Libra is always open to an agreeable suggestion. Just be careful that if you use the word "great" you mean it. And smile.

What's important to you in the evaluation of a restaurant?

> I like it when the tables are far enough apart so that you can speak softly and be heard.

What new trends on the restaurant scene don't you like?

> I hate restaurants with names like discos—Samples, Tingles, Waffles, Truffles, Chuckles, Pimples....

> I don't like this ragin' cajun BS—throwing pepper all over everything and calling it "cajun delight."

Romantic Menus for Libra

To romance him:

Table: a candle
Appetizer: unnecessary
Soup: French onion with melted gruyère
Entrée: shrimp and veal sauté; steamed asparagus
Wine: knows that wine and asparagus don't mix (he tastefully suggests
    vodka tonics)
Dessert: strawberries and Grand Marnier; coffee

To romance her:

Table: fruit and nut muffins (fresh from the oven), butter
Appetizer: unnecessary
Soup: unnecessary
Entrée: medley of lobster, chicken and tortellini salads; fresh fruit garnish
Wine: Fumé Blanc versus Pinot Grigio (She'll love the opportunity to com-
    pare two wines and choose.)
Dessert: chocolate gelato and imported butter cookies; coffee

Libra Food Fantasy

The Libra requires romance, and romance requires a setting: a picnic blanket in a mountain meadow; a candlelit table with a view of the ocean; room service in a grand hotel.

The Libra requires romance, and romance requires nourishment: French foods and fine wines; burgers and milkshakes; potato chips and champagne.

The Libra requires romance, and romance requires a partner: a beautiful woman; a handsome man; something in between.

While this is a basic fantasy for all of the signs, it has more of the air of a practical goal to the Libra. This may well be the Libra's greatest contribution to human endeavor—the belief that love must seek a kindred spirit. If one can't be responsive to all people or all behavior, reasons the Libra, one must still seek out at least one other person with whom to share love.

But if true romantic love is a tangible goal to Libras, then what is their fantasy?

Sometimes, like Libra president Jimmy Carter, they sin in their hearts. But ironically, the Libra even more frequently fantasizes being left alone in the solitary pursuit of something uncompromisingly beautiful. To play a perfect round of golf at Pebble Beach, to have work hung in a Santa Fe gallery, to prepare a delightful meal in Paris: these are the dreams of Libran self-expression.

Nothing crappy. Ever.

Who would be your ideal fantasy companion for dinner?

I don't know. I don't admire too many people. I'm not a star worshipper.

What would be your idea of the perfect meal?

Chicken salad in pita on a beautiful beach by myself.

Quick Fried Rice

submitted by Thomas Shreyer

1 lb. bacon
6 eggs
1 fresh onion
3 cups Minute Rice (butter and salt)
soy sauce

Prepair [*sic*—in a very Libra sort of way] rice and put onion in with rice. You can add other spices if desired. Cut bacon to bite size and fry. Remove bacon from pan. Scramble eggs in grease till eggs are mostly browned (almost burn). Add rice back to pan with eggs and add bacon, then soy sauce. Fry part of rice to crispy crust, then stir.

Eggs in a Basket

submitted independently by Libras Carol Carlson, of Philadelphia, and Briggs Hubbel, of Phoenix!

Punch a hole in a piece of bread with a baking powder can. Fry an egg in the hole.

[Note: several Libras also mentioned a fondness for making sliced and deviled hard-boiled eggs.]

Vegetables for Grilled Foods

submitted by Marty Lieberman

Chop and dice an onion. Brown it. Put in all sorts of s—: wine, soy sauce, worcestershire sauce. Add green pepper and mushrooms, butter and garlic salt, and whatever else seems good at the time.

If I can't grill it, I can't cook it.

Spinach Salad

submitted by Maureen Logan

It's just fresh spinach, sliced mushrooms, sliced scallions, crumbled bleu cheese, oil and vinegar and pepper.

Filets de Sole Pescatore

submitted by Andrew Whiley

22 oz. fresh sole cut into strips
(finger size)
4 oz. fresh mussels, cooked, beard
removed (reserve juice)
5 oz. skinned, seeded tomatoes
1 lb. cooked fresh spinach

1 clove garlic
1 oz. chopped onion
1 egg
bread crumbs
3 oz. butter
2 oz. smoked salmon

Toss spinach in butter, season with salt, pepper and nutmeg, and arrange in the middle of a long dish. Coat strips of sole with egg and bread crumbs, deep fry and dress them on the spinach, leaving a free space in the center. Sauté the onions in butter, add crushed garlic and tomatoes, season and simmer, then add the mussels. Fill this mixture in the middle of the fillets. Sauté the smoked salmon in butter and scatter over the top of the dish. Make a cream sauce from the mussel juice, season with herbs and border the spinach with it.

Cinnamon Chicken

submitted by Basia Lubicz

3-1/2 lb. chicken, cut into serving
pieces
1 clove garlic, bruised
4 T. butter, melted
1 t. cinnamon

1 tablespoon soy sauce
1/4 cup white wine
1 t. sugar
chopped fresh parsley

Heat the oven to 400°. Rub the chicken pieces well with the bruised garlic. Pour the melted butter into a baking dish. Roll the chicken in the butter to coat each piece. Turn the chicken skin side up in the pan and dust each piece with cinnamon and sprinkle with soy sauce. Bake the chicken for 30 minutes.

Reduce the heat to 350°. Sprinkle the chicken with white wine and then the sugar. Bake the chicken until the juices run clear when pricked with a fork, about 1/2 hour longer. Garnish with chopped parsley. Serves four.

My Favorite Recipe

submitted by Donna Chase

The phone number of any of my husband's restaurants.

Baked Scrod Provencale

submitted by Nancy Weiss

2 oz. olive oil
2 oz. sliced red onion
2 oz. diced celery
1 t. crushed garlic
12 oz. diced peeled tomatoes
1 oz. tomato paste
1/3 cup dry white wine
1/2 cup clam juice

1/2 oz. chopped fresh parsley
1 t. oregano
1/2 t. thyme
1/2 t. grated orange peel
1/2 t. salt
a dash of ground black pepper
a dash of cayenne
6 6-oz. scrod fillets

Sauté onion, celery and garlic in oil until limp. Add tomatoes, tomato paste, wine and clam juice; bring to boil, then reduce to simmer. Add remaining ingredients, except for fish, and cook for 15-20 minutes. Place individual fillets in separate casserole dishes and cover each with 2 to 3 ounces of hot sauce. Bake in 425° oven for approximately 10 minutes, until fish barely begins to flake. Serve with garlic toast and a green salad.

Some Libra Food Personalities

I'm sure there are thousands of Libra food personalities out there, but I failed to come up with a single household name. Certainly, no slight is intended. I am prepared to receive, although their natures make it highly unlikely I'll get, Libra hate mail on the subject.

Otherwise, if you're looking for an exceptional dining experience in Phoenix, Arizona, try Vincent Guerithault's place on Camelback Road. He's a Libra.

So is Chris Inden, a wonderful chef and friend who is now an executive for a big food service corporation, and who was once selected to be the pope's personal chef in Chicago.

"We both wear white as a sign of purity," the pontiff told Chris.

My ex-wife, Nancy, who when I last heard was cooking in New York City at a restaurant called Arizona 206, is also a Libra. I'm sure she's not hurting the place any (unless she's trying to make waffles).

Scorpio

October 23 to November 22

Talk about meat and drink! To see that man lying there as dead as a herring filled me full.

Robert Louis Stevenson (Scorpio), author
from "The Beach of Falesa"

What ten foods would I take to a deserted island? Fish, pasta, chocolate, green beans—that's it, that's all I eat. But I'm not going anywhere I have to be alone. I'd rather starve than not have company.

Lisa Harryman (Scorpio), property manager

Scorpios, who do not like their inner workings to be presented for public consideration, are already reading this with concern. What's this guy saying? That we eat live flesh and drink warm blood?

As anyone even passingly familiar with astrology knows, Scorpios are characterized by their personal intensity. Some astrologers treat Scorpios as no less than human atomic bombs—silent, armed, a little crazy and incredibly dangerous. Well, with Scorpio it isn't hard to go to extremes.

A Scorpio's life matches the power of the human will against a universe of mortal obstacles and challenges. Scorpios are whatever-it-takes survivalists. They thrive on heavy confrontation, the proving grounds of the will, and are more than justly associated with the power struggles of barrooms, bedrooms, battlefields and boardrooms.

Scorpios' greatest need, for ill and for good, is to have their inner mastery sincerely acknowledged and rewarded by others. This is different from simply demanding a cautious respect for their power. A Scorpio can be incredibly mild, thoughtful and kind, but even this sort of behavior is tendered with an expectation of restitution for loving services rendered.

Perhaps they are right. Life can only provide so much to so many. Why be more of a patsy than is absolutely ordained?

But really now—they are in fact human, and even put their pants on (or, more appropriate to Scorpio, take them off) the proverbial one leg at a time. They do laugh if the joke is funny. And they have to eat.

In fact, most Scorpios love to eat. There's a lot of public and private passion for the subject of dining, and many Scorpios are professionally involved in food-related careers. The food world offers ample opportunities for people and task management, financial gain, strong sensory experiences and influence over one of life's true necessities, and that's a hard combination for the Scorpio to resist.

When it comes to specific food preferences, Scorpios generally favor the intense. They go for foods that are salty (bacon products, caviar), dairy-rich (melted cheese toppings, pastries), astringent (pickles, peppermint), effervescent (Classic Coke, seltzer) and well-spiced (peasant cuisines, particularly Italian). They are drawn to the classic aphrodisiacs (oysters, pepper), have an odd incidence of red-colored foods among their favorites (tomato sauce, red pepper, corned beef, pickled beets, raspberries) and are singularly unfond of fruit (a little too mild and sweet for their natures).

Scorpios have a pronounced tendency to view even simple enterprises as serious competitions (try to get one to return a telephone call promptly), so they are naturally strict in the evaluation of their own and other's culinary endeavors. They are not just concerned with the way a dish tastes, but also with the skill with which it was prepared and served. A particular sticking point is that a dish arrive at table timed to the exact moment of doneness, at the appropriate serving temperature and with the appropriate utensils already placed.

In restaurants, Scorpio will fume at high prices if absolutely fair value has not been given. Price gouging is robbery and assault to Scorpio and will not be politely waived off. With money, as with all instruments of power, one should tread warily with Scorpio.

These people may not actually drink blood—but they do have a way of going out after it.

Do you eat out often?

Well, what do you mean by often?

What do you usually eat for lunch?

Cheese crisps, pita pizzas, special nachos—sandwiches. I like assertive, spicy flavors.

Who is your favorite companion for dinner?

Anybody who'll pick up the check.

Ten Foods a Scorpio Needs to Survive on a Deserted Island

Cheese • Italian bread • Milk • Chicken • Chocolate
Eggs • Water • Tomatoes • Pasta • Broccoli

What ten foods would you want on a deserted island?

Can you boil sea water to make it fresh? Can I catch my own fish?

Scorpio Island

It is a place where each level of reality conceals another, a chain of mysteries for a constantly deepening perception. So one may see the seashore but not the hidden reefs. So one may encounter the hidden reefs but fail to fathom the secret life within.

There are many fences and boundaries on Scorpio Island, and good strong locks on the doors. Wild underbrush defines, guards and encroaches upon carefully tended vegetable gardens. In sturdy tool sheds weapons are at the ready.

Gardens and guns are emblems of Scorpio self-reliance. These people like to be involved in raising some of their own food when possible, as this helps to guarantee uninterrupted supply and purity of source. Weapons are useful agents for extending the menu, as well as for discouraging competition for resources.

Inside the Scorpio homes there is a sense of solidity and safety, if not of unmitigated light and warmth. Scorpios favor durability over style, and select materials and furnishings on the basis of strength in construction or as they symbolically suggest experiences where power has prevailed (hunting trophies, animal skin rugs and heavy tactile sculptures may abound). Cooking is a serious function in these homes, and there is frequently restaurant-grade or cast iron equipment in the kitchen, along with evidence of devotion to the "pure" culinary techniques of history such as brick-oven baking and hardwood smoking.

Commercial areas abound on Scorpio Island, nor do these generally reflect modern times. The dominant structures look like old bank buildings and mercantile exchanges, and are guaranteed to have smoke-filled sanctums and massive treasure-filled vaults. Luncheons and suppers are taken in traditional club dining rooms and conservative employee cafeterias where business is conducted in deceptively quiet tones punctuated with perceptive chewing and portentous swallows.

There are a small handful of truly inspired restaurants on Scorpio Island, where food quality, service, atmosphere and value come together in exceptional testimony to competence and beauty. These are regarded by the natives as "occasion" places, however, which the Scorpios rarely patronize just for the sake of enjoyment, particularly if they are paying. On the other hand, the island is rife with weather-beaten skid row joints, where the natives can frequently be found flirting with ptomaine and temptation. Perhaps surprisingly, the local Wendy's also does a pretty good business, perhaps because of its comparatively adult menu and decor.

For all this, few people ever discover all the secret spots of Scorpio Island. What's there? Maybe a Transylvanian-style castle or a medieval monastery. Likely a nuclear missile silo. If you're thinking about going, it's suggested you mind your manners with the natives and pack your own lunch.

What's a good restaurant to bring the kids to?

I like adult menus with kid-portion prices. I respect a place that doesn't make you stay home just because you have kids. Mine know how to behave.

Scorpio Favorites

Vegetable: broccoli
Fruit: raspberries
Starch: pasta
Source of protein: dairy products
Bread product: crusty Italian bread
Dairy product: all
Spice or herb: basil, oregano, pepper
Condiment: cocktail sauce
Ice cream flavor: chocolate
Pizza topping: pepperoni
Candy: Butterfinger
Cookie: chocolate chip

Sandwich: bacon-lettuce-tomato on
   toasted sour rye
Soup: chowder
Soft drink: Classic Coke
Beer: Heineken
Wine: hearty red
Liquor: premium whiskey
Liqueur: Irish Cream, brandy
Comfort food: spaghetti
Celebration food: lobster
Junk food: hamburgers
Sexy food: caviar, oysters

What is your favorite fruit?

The only fruit I eat is bananas. Maybe also two apples a year.

What is your favorite sandwich?

I like the hoagies at the Wawa's. Seven ounces of meat is a good value at the price.

What is your favorite condiment?

Lemon, more than anything else, improves the flavor of food.

What is your favorite junk food?

Coca-Cola. But I blame that on my husband.

Scorpio Diet and Health

The Scorpio's attitude about dieting can be easily anticipated. If you need to lose weight, you should starve yourself. The more it hurts, the more successful the diet.

Exercising willpower is Scorpios' fundamental approach to all matters of health and diet. These people have a legendary capacity for self-control and a near-miraculous ability to heal themselves of the most debilitating physical conditions. Frequently they can even accomplish feats of healing for others—a fact that sounds a little hyperbolic until it is personally encountered (and at the very least, it should be noted that there are many doctors and dentists born under this sign).

What is perhaps surprising is that one does encounter plenty of over-weight smokers among the ranks of Scorpios. Here it seems fair analysis to reiterate the passionate characteristics of the Scorpio, and to note how this may turn to girth or a chain-smoking habit when other outlets for release are denied. A Scorpio failing to get his due can become very hungry.

With Scorpios, though, one is tempted to think that they add pounds just for the painful pleasure of trying to shed them. Scorpios' desire for intense experience is satisfied both by over-indulgence and by atonement for over-indulgence. All diets, as attempts at self-mastery and physical transformation, partake of the nature of the scorpion.

What one should keep in mind with Scorpio is that it is intensely satisfying for them to cause someone else to go off a diet. It's just another contest of wills to them. You are warned here that the foods Scorpios most often love to cook for others are rich desserts, big breakfasts and holiday meals.

If you need to prove to the Scorpio that you are a dieting force to be reckoned with, start talking about fiber. Scorpio is said to rule all processes of elimination, and one of Scorpios' personal dietary secrets is to scrub themselves out with roughage and fiber. This may sound a little like Virgo, but we're talking *level* of participation here.

It's like that old gross joke about elephants:

Q. What do you give a constipated Scorpio?

A: Plenty of room.

Do you ever diet? How?

> Yes. I eat lots of bran cereal and drink warm water. It works.

> Uh huh. Strength of will.

Ten More Foods Scorpios Like a Whole Lot

Pizza • Peanut butter • Cream cheese • Rice • Spinach
Asparagus • Wine • Berries • Ham • Red peppers

Things You Should Not Feed a Scorpio

Fruit-flavored anything
Failed culinary experiments

What are some foods or flavors that turn you off?

> Liver makes me gag.

Scorpio Homefood

Consider the power of controlling the food supply and you begin to perceive the attraction of the kitchen to Scorpio. A Scorpio understands that anyone who brings home or fries up the bacon is entitled to lay down some laws. Their family food responsibilities are not held lightly.

A Scorpio cook not only feeds the family, but monitors moods and manners through an enforced schedule of meal times. Teenagers and their Scorpio parents frequently have a rough go of it, as the Scorpio expects everyone to report in for what amounts to a multi-level inspection. The Scorpio treats domestic dining as a family management tool.

One indicator of Scorpios' domestic managerial competence is that these people always seem to have well-stocked refrigerators and cupboards. Scorpios are forever making solid meals out of leftovers, which they plan into their culinary efforts. These people just don't leave themselves very vulnerable, even when it comes to having something readily available for lunch.

Ask Scorpios about dining memories from their own childhood and they remember the family "power" meals; mother's feats of provision and endurance at Thanksgiving or Christmas; big Sunday dinners of lasagna, roast beef and mashed potatoes, homemade breads and cakes.

Not surprisingly, the Scorpio likes to prepare and partake of the same meals as an adult. In addition to the ample and flavorful foods of these occasions, Scorpios have deep respect for the enduring quality of ritual gatherings. In the case of a major holiday feast they can be quite fussy about making sure that certain dishes and customs are repeated exactly from year to year.

While the Scorpio is among the most technically competent of cooks and has a decided bias towards flavorful foods, there is sometimes a bit of an Achilles heel when it comes to imagination in the kitchen. Many Scorpios profess to being interested in cooking as a creative outlet, but most Scorpio cooks have a derivative culinary repertoire. In true Scorpio fashion, many of their favorite recipes are time-tested "secrets," obtained from sources such as grandmothers, old cookbooks or friends who happen to be professional chefs.

Whatever their objective culinary talents and liabilities, Scorpios almost always favor eating at home to eating out. Considering that they are often their own toughest critics, there is definitely a lot of persevering energy that goes into a Scorpio's domestic culinary life. Of course it's all worth it to the Scorpios, who thereby make themselves less vulnerable to all those incompetent rip-off restaurateurs waiting out there to poison, rob and otherwise assault them.

A Scorpio will hardly ever poison a family member, unless their teenager gets a little too careless about curfew.

What's the most interesting thing in your refrigerator?

Fresh fruit. I hate it.

Was your mother a good cook?

No, but my dad had a lot of food allergies so it wasn't her fault.
When I went to college I couldn't understand why everyone else thought dorm food was so bad.

Scorpio Breakfast

A preoccupied Scorpio may entirely ignore breakfast, but most have some affection and respect for traditional morning fare. Aware of the requirements of system maintenance, they appreciate the virtues of whole grains and fresh citrus pulp, and understand the carbohydrate/energy connection (although they are not into very sweet products). For protein and taste, Scorpios love dairy products and are extremely fond of the saltiness encountered in breakfast meats.

Any special-occasion breakfast can really get a Scorpio's juices flowing. Along with family holiday gatherings, Scorpios enthusiastically embrace business breakfasts and "morning after" breakfast affairs. In such situations, the Scorpio is a master at using the niceties of the meal to deflect attention from the purposeful character-probing and dealing that is actually going on. Pay particular attention if Bloody Marys are suggested.

Thankfully, not everything in a Scorpio's life is a *massive* confrontation. There's a particularly genuine niceness to a Scorpio parent having breakfast with a small child, as the former dispenses valuable insight and the latter contributes meaningful feedback. Scorpios believe that children, who are not generally power threats, are very often better company than other adults, naturally wiser and more honest. Their own children in particular.

Who is your favorite companion for breakfast?

My lover from the night before.

Who would you select as a fantasy companion for breakfast?

Mikhail Baryshnikov. And I don't care if he can make an omelet.

As a fantasy companion for breakfast? For lunch? For dinner?

Burt Reynolds. Burt. The Big B.

Scorpio Breakfast Favorites

Juices: grapefruit, V-8
Fruits: grapefruit, strawberries with sour cream
Cereals: Shredded Wheat, oatmeal
Sweet rolls: not usually interested
Bread: English muffins
Egg dish: cheese and bacon omelets
Other: Bloody Marys

Scorpio Awayfood

When a Scorpio describes an absolutely favorite restaurant, the terms used include "fantastic," "best," "beautiful," "lovely" and "genuine." Now consider that no one avoids false praise or hyperbole more than Scorpio, and also consider that fewer people are generally less fond of dining out, and you appreciate that when a Scorpio uses any favorable adjective it is certainly more than richly deserved.

The truth, though, is that while Scorpios may occasionally enjoy dining out as a forum for human encounter and even relaxation, they are not really fond of a great many restaurants. What particularly turns them off is any sign of inept or careless management and, considering the Scorpios' powers of scrutiny, such discovery is not often difficult. Also, in a broad sense, Scorpios feel that paying a triple or quadruple mark-up for raw food that has merely been combined and cooked by some unseen felon (Scorpios are big fans of open display kitchens in restaurants) amounts to highway robbery.

If you want to impress a Scorpio, do not go to the glitziest restaurant in town (unless you are very much in your element and price is no object). Scorpios enjoy being spoiled, but blatant attempts at seduction are doomed to failure. When the game is "trying to impress," they will not come cheaply.

What will turn Scorpios on is your very favorite secret joint—a romantic neighborhood Italian restaurant or a great bar with cheesy appetizers and an even cheesier crowd. Under no circumstances, however, should they be placed in overtly hostile environments—unless, that is, you can use a knife for more than buttering bread.

Scorpios like a good restaurant brunch, especially when they are on vacation and dining seems an especially valid activity. They are happiest at buffets, where they can serve themselves and eat all they want for a fixed price, thereby insuring a modicum of safety and value. They are usually fond of salad bars for the same reasons, and are even more enthusiastic when local fresh produce is featured.

Remember that if a Scorpio invites you out to a restaurant and uses any positive adjective in its description, you should enthusiastically accept the invitation. If the term used is something like "great" or "fantastic," start getting ready immediately. The place will be special beyond words.

How do you decide to try a restaurant you've never been to before?

Usually recommendation. I hate to try a shot in the dark.

What new trends in the restaurant scene don't you like?

Higher prices.

What is your favorite restaurant entrée?

Fish. My theme is "fish is an aphrodisiac."

Romantic Menus for Scorpio

To romance him:

Table: expensive conservative appointments
Appetizer: baked clams oreganato
Salad: spinach with hot bacon dressing
Entrée: rack of lamb; baked tomatoes; rice pilaf
Wine: hearty French red
Dessert: chocolate mousse; brandy and coffee

To romance her:

Table: strong tactile statements (e.g. nubby linen; polished table statuary)
Appetizer: chile con queso with tortilla chips
Soup: minestrone with fresh fennel and hot sausage
Entrée: baked potato with poached egg, caviar and sour cream
Wine: Burgundy
Dessert: chocolate-dipped strawberries with whipped cream; Irish cream
    liqueur

What's a sexy food?

　　That's a dumb question. I'm a Scorpio.

Scorpio Food Fantasy

Not one Scorpio interviewed could be persuaded to reveal this secret in any depth. It was like asking professional gamblers to reveal their hole cards. There was, however, some mention of waiters in g-strings, vast quantities of whipped cream and expensive cognac. And one young Scorpio respondent did write her phone number at this point on the questionnaire—but I'm sworn to secrecy, which I've the good sense to keep.

Oyster and Spinach Bisque

submitted by Mary E. King

1 medium onion, chopped fine
2 cloves garlic, chopped fine
1 stick butter
1 10-oz. package frozen spinach,
　　chopped
1 pint oysters and juice

1/3 cup flour
2 cups half and half
2 cups heavy cream
1 T. chicken base or 2 bouillon
　　cubes dissolved in 1/4 cup water
salt and white pepper

Melt half the butter in large pot. Sauté onion and garlic in butter. Add oysters and sauté till edges curl. Melt remaining butter in pan, stir in flour to make a roux, stirring till smooth. Add roux to onion and oysters. When it begins to boil, add half and half, cream, spinach and chicken base. Cook till spinach is done, but do not let boil. Stir frequently. Season with salt and pepper to taste. This dish is extraordinary!

Quesadillas

submitted by Ann P. Brody

2 flour tortillas
1/2 cup grated cheese (jack or cheddar or both)
3 pieces sun-dried tomatoes, thinly sliced
pickled jalapeños, sliced (optional)
3 slices bacon, cooked and crumbled
1 scallion, thinly sliced

Preheat a heavy skillet over medium heat. Spread the cheese over one tortilla. Top with the rest of the ingredients and cover with the other tortilla. Grill in a dry skillet until browned on one side. Turn and continue cooking until browned on the other side and the cheese melts. Cut in wedges with a pizza cutter. Great snack or lunch. (Smoked ham or other meat can be substituted for bacon.)

Shrimp Covered in Chocolate

submitted by Lisa Harryman

You dip it.

Olive Salsa Verde

submitted by Kris Ostlund

2 cups chopped parsley
1/3 cup finely diced onion
1/4 cup chopped mild salt-cured
   olives (Italian Ponentine olives
   are perfect and can be found in
   specialty shops and delis)

1 T. capers, chopped
1/4 T. fresh lemon juice
1 T. fresh lime juice
zest of one lemon, chopped
1 large clove of garlic, chopped finely
1/2 cup olive oil (approximately)

Chop parsley, onion, olives, capers, lemon zest, and garlic. Place in a stainless steel bowl. Add lemon and lime juice. Slowly add olive oil. The mixture should be slightly runny, however not so loose that it will run off the meat it is served on. Place two tablespoons of the olive salsa verde on grilled chicken breast or grilled pork. Serves six. Serve with Inglenook Napa Valley Estate Bottled 1983 Sauvignon Blanc.

Chicken Divan

submitted by Darlene Minnemyer

3 10-oz. packages frozen broccoli
   spears
6 chicken breasts, cooked
3 cans cream of chicken soup
1-1/2 cups mayonnaise

1/3 cup shredded processed
   American cheese
1/3 cup shredded parmesan cheese
1/3 cup sliced almonds

Boil broccoli about three minutes and drain. Remove chicken from bone and cut in large pieces. Mix soup, mayonnaise and American cheese together well. Arrange broccoli in a baking dish and place chicken over the top. Pour soup mixture over chicken. Sprinkle with parmesan cheese and almonds. Bake at 350° for 25-30 minutes. Serves four to six.

Blarney Stones

submitted by Myriel Hiner

Cut a sponge cake into rectangles. Frost with powdered sugar, butter, vanilla and cream icing. Roll in crushed peanuts (all sides).

Butterscotch Bon Bons

submitted by Marcie Beert

1 cup butterscotch chips
1 cup peanut butter
1-1/2 cups miniature marshmallows
1-1/2 cups corn flakes

Melt chips in microwave oven or double boiler; add peanut butter. Remove from heat. Add marshmallows and corn flakes. Drop by teaspoonfuls on waxed papered cookie sheets. Refrigerate.

Lemon Cottage Puddings

submitted by Charlotte Walker

1 cup sugar
1/4 cup all-purpose flour
1/4 t. salt
3 large eggs, separated

1 cup half and half
freshly grated zest of 1 lemon
1/3 cup fresh lemon juice

Preheat oven to 375°. In a medium bowl combine sugar, flour and salt. In a separate bowl, whisk egg yolks, half and half, lemon zest and lemon juice to blend. Whisk in sugar mixture. In a third bowl, beat egg whites until soft moist peaks form. Stir one-fourth of whites into batter to lighten it; fold in remaining whites. Divide batter among eight 1/2-cup soufflé dishes or individual charlotte molds. Set in large baking dish containing about one inch hot water. Bake 25 to 30 minutes, until puddings are set and tops are browned. Serves eight. You can serve these hot or chilled.

Some Scorpio Food Personalities

Auguste Escoffier, father of classic French cooking
Jane and Michael Stern (born two days apart), food-interest authors
Jan Weimer, food editor, *Bon Appétit*

Sagittarius

November 23 to December 21

"Has he asked for anything special?"

"Yes, this morning for breakfast he requested something called wheat germ, organic honey and tiger's milk."

"Oh yes, those are the charmed substances that some years ago were felt to contain life-preserving properties."

"You mean there was no deep fat, no steak, or cream pies or hot fudge?"

"Those were thought to be unhealthy, precisely the opposite of what we now know to be true."

"Incredible."

Woody Allen (Sagittarius), screen writer
from the movie *Sleeper*

My favorite condiment is South America.

John Gamble (Sagittarius), marketing executive

Sagittarius is as close as the zodiac gets to an omnivore. Not only do Sagittarians believe variety to be the spice of life, they also feel it yields much of the substance. In all areas of existence, very definitely including diet, the fundamental Sagittarian qualities are expansion and insight—Sagittarians feel a strong need to go everywhere and at first-hand to get to the heart of everything.

Ultimately, it is the Sagittarius who is the true gastronome. Without undue emotional involvement or compulsive attitudes, a Sagittarius regards food with a profound sense of discovery and enjoyment. No other sign better combines a sense of the necessity of eating with a vast sense of enthusiasm for dining's diverse fun and adventure.

Inclined to a life of travel and philosophical breadth, the Sagittarius has eaten Chinese food in Peking, French food in Paris and Wyoming food in Cheyenne, and is a true champion of all the world's great culinary expressions of soulfulness. At the same time, there is no one who will more enthusiastically regard a Twinkie or a snow cone, and Sagittarians are often as equally fond of canned diet soda as they are devoted to fine wine. "I like everything," is their menu mantra.

Sometimes they seem totally without discretion or control in dietary matters. They'll manifest interest in nutrition, then they'll eat their weight in cheesecake. They'll brilliantly appraise novel flavor combinations on a menu, then order a ham and cheese sandwich. They'll espouse the most praiseworthy moral codes, then have one more for the road.

Much is revealed in the Sagittarian symbol, the centaur, half divine hunter and half horse's rear end. Sagittarians will zero in on and digest life's most subtle and all-encompassing truths, and then bestially expel them at the most inappropriate moments. Long on true understanding, they can be most short on tact.

To appreciate them, though, is to understand their insatiable appetite for experience and observation. Deeply devoted to the pursuit of human wisdom, they are not capable of the blind credulity of faith. Sagittarians must make their own mistakes, live their own triumphs and draw their own conclusions.

Whatever else one charges Sagittarius with, there is no denying the sign's earnest search for that which matters in human experience. They have no prejudice in this ambition, and they never undervalue a sense of humor in the effort. They are willing to chase some luck, but they know wisdom is always hard won.

Ironically, Sagittarians have particularly great fondness for apples—like the one from the Tree of Knowledge, and the one that inspired Johnny Appleseed's journeys, and the one William Tell shot at, and the one that gets the horse once more around the track. Their favorite apples, though, are the non-metaphorical variety, served in an excellent warm tart with lots of vanilla ice cream or a wedge of cheddar on the side. They won't turn down the McDonald's version either.

How preoccupied are you with the subjects of food and dining?

That's an easy question to answer. On a scale of one to ten, I'd have to say eleven.

What new trends on the dining scene don't you like?

I hate small portions. I enjoy an eating heritage. When I was growing up, if you finished everything, there wasn't enough served.

Ten Foods a Sagittarian Needs to Survive on a Deserted Island

Prime rib • Pasta specialties • Apples • Fine wine • Natural cheeses
Tomatoes • Specialty breads with butter • Chicken • Water
Baked potatoes with everything

What ten foods would you need to survive on a deserted island?

If it's food, I want it there.

Sounds like fun.

I love to eat.

I'm dismayed at so short a list. I hate being limited.

Help!

Sagittarius Island

It is a stimulating compilation of environments—hermitical mountain retreat, complex urban downtown, progressive suburban neighborhood, weathered university cloister, daredevil amusement park, combination fishing village and seaside resort. Everywhere are facilities for the purposes of education and recreation. And of every conceivable variety, of every nationality and price/value orientation, there are restaurants.

Most familiar to the eye are the many chains and fast food establishments, including a number of Burger Kings (most Sagittarians are convinced that flame-broiling is superior) *and* McDonald's (the best breakfast sandwich). But there is also every other kind of dining option imaginable, from ding-a-ling ice cream trucks to the most exalted temples of gastronomy. And, in each and every one of the specialized environments, there is at least one particularly wonderful place that weaves an almost magical web of appropriate atmosphere, attendant food expression and honest hospitality.

For the home cook, there are myriad places to shop for ingredients, including many ethnic specialty stores, gourmet wine and cheese shops and roadside orchard stands. For the most part, though, the Sagittarius likes to patronize the island's super-colossal grocery store. Sagittarians love big open areas and variety, so they usually love the modern "miles of aisles" approach to food retailing.

In short, it would not be off-base to appraise Sagittarius Island as a place where the enjoyment of food is a major part of life. In fact, there is only one other type of commercial institution on Sagittarius Island encountered with any more frequency than food emporiums.

Travel agencies.

Sagittarians truly do not like the idea of confinement. A life spent totally on an island, even of one's own fantasizing, would be the closest thing to a Sagittarius' living hell. And that's why the busiest place on Sagittarius Island is the airport (which has a very decent little snack bar that serves an excellent chili dog).

Where do you like to shop for food?

I hate shopping, it's my worst chore. I'm a bitch. It's because I'm in a service-oriented business and I feel you don't get good service in a food store. I hate the candy traps for little kids. I'd rather do laundry. Really, Kevin has to go with me to calm me down.

What do you generally eat for lunch?

I never eat lunch, just yogurt and an apple at my desk. Lunch ruins my work day. It slows me down and I can't get my snap back.

Sagittarian Favorites

Vegetable: asparagus
Fruit: apples
Starch: all
Source of protein: all, including beans and cheese
Bread product: whole wheat, egg bread
Dairy product: cheese, yogurt
Spice or herb: basil, garlic
Condiment: ketchup
Ice cream flavor: vanilla with assorted toppings
Pizza topping: everything: extra cheese, hot peppers and anchovies
Candy: chocolate-covered mints
Cookie: homemade peanut butter, oatmeal raisin

Sandwich: grilled sausage and cheese on toasted rye
Soup: gazpacho
Soft drink: diet soda
Beer: Budweiser
Wine: premium varietal
Liquor: bourbon, vodka
Liqueur: B & B
Comfort food : chicken or beef with noodles, Oreos
Celebration food: turkey
Junk food: nachos
Sexy food: champagne, seafood appetizers

What's your favorite celebration food?

My wife's a restaurant critic. A celebration is when I get to choose what we're having.

What's your favorite comfort food?

Peanut butter on everything at certain times of the month.

What's your favorite beverage?

Iced tea over the long haul, although Jack Daniels also figures large in my life.

Sagittarius Diet and Health

Nutrition is too important a topic not to register in the Sagittarian awareness. Even though they may understand the value of a moderate balanced diet consisting of healthy wholesome foods, however, Sagittarians are not always prone to the practice. Heck, dieting and cutting down on favorite foods is just not any fun—and what if, as Sagittarian Woody Allen suggests, the nutritionists are someday proven wrong?

All that wasted opportunity for deep fat and hot fudge!

Almost all Sagittarians, even if not currently overweight, can tell you about the time they were fat. A Sagittarian on a roll is a four milkshake per day kind of guy (or gal). The lines between meals and snacks get completely blurred.

Usually, Sagittarians will eventually pull back from obesity as the negative social and health ramifications become apparent. They learn to adapt to fewer meal periods (Sagittarians are frequent breakfast or lunch skippers), because their restraint once at table is always tenuous. Sagittarians just dearly love to see things expand, and are the zodiac's most fervent worshippers in the cult of the carbohydrate (even beyond consumption, just watching pasta, rice or bread grow as it cooks is a turn-on to them).

Sagittarians compensate for abundant intake by being one of the zodiac's most physically active signs. These people are avid exercise and sports enthusiasts. For most Sagittarians, a diet is totally worthless unless it entails a stepped-up physical regimen.

Where the Sagittarian approach to diet and health is particularly interesting is in the area of ethical considerations. Quite a few Sagittarians become vegetarians at some point in their lives, not for health reasons, but in the sincere belief that it is wrong to kill animals for food. Similarly, a Sagittarius will almost always consider generous hospitality to be more essential to satisfactory dining than good nutrition—wholesomeness and balance are great, but goodwill and large portions are essential.

Do you diet?

> Oh yeah, every night. Then I go off the diet in the morning. I lose forty pounds, I gain it back.

Do you have any nutritional habits or beliefs?

> I used to take vitamins but I stopped because they didn't taste good.

> Never eat anything that has a cleansing function in an animal.

Ten More Foods Most Sagittarians Like a Whole Lot

Ice cream • Diet soda • Italian food • Chinese food • Mexican food Greek food • Japanese food • Indian food • Thai food Regional specialties

Things You Should Not Feed a Sagittarius

Foods with monochromatic flavors
Very bitter foods

What are some foods or flavors that turn you off?

> I never seem to have that problem.

Sagittarius Homefood

Mothers of young Sagittarians quickly learn that the only way to keep their kids around the house is to feed them. Otherwise mom gets to know only the pile of cosmic debris left in the Sagittarian's wake. This pile usually contains a lot of athletic paraphernalia, a lot of reading material and a lot of food wrappers.

Probably those same moms would be surprised by both the fondness and accuracy with which their cooking is remembered by their grown children. Sagittarians are always appreciative of their mom's best dishes, and many potato latkes, chicken paprikashes, lasagnas, pot pies and banana puddings are counted among a Sagittarian's finest memories of home.

As cooks themselves, Sagittarians spend a lot of time "improving" the casseroles and stews they first learned at home. Sagittarians covet a wide range of experiences when they dine out, but in cooking for themselves, family and friends they are much more likely to provide a flavorful meat loaf than a fancy *filet de boeuf.* Actually, they most enjoy producing "spreads"— both in terms of putting out large platters with large portions, and in terms of serving an assortment of main dishes with a lot of interesting sauces and condiments.

A single Sagittarian is likely to be a pillar of the convenience food industry (if a Sagittarian tells you that one variety of canned minestrone tastes superior to another, you can be certain it's true), but there will most always be some flavor or ingredient embellishment made to the food that comes out of a can or box. In fairness, this same single Sagittarian will also be quite capable of cooking up something special from scratch in the name of romance, often brilliantly authentic taste treats matched with expertly chosen libations.

Ultimately, cooking is creative play to the Sagittarius. It's one of life's few activities in which something can be addressed that's simultaneously fun, interesting, attractive, and functional. It's a game you get to eat.

Was your mother a good cook?

Fair. Here's a woman who owned a farm and couldn't cook a steak. But she was great with Jell-O.

Do you like to cook?

I enjoy it. It's like putting together an erector set.

What's your favorite kitchen gadget or piece of cooking equipment?

The microwave oven, and scissors for the bags.

What is the most interesting thing in your refrigerator?

Some herbed mustard I brought back from France. It's goose-shit green.

Sagittarius Breakfast

Sagittarians are usually pretty quick to get started in the morning, and their approach to breakfast will generally go one of two ways:

They may be dieting, in which case they must delay their first consideration of food as far into the day as possible. The first snack and they're doomed. Many of these Sagittarians are likely to grab juice, coffee and vitamins, if anything, then head on over for an early workout at the gym.

The other Sagittarian is not generally a breakfast lingerer either, but there is a stop in the pantry. Sagittarians love breakfast cereals, and they love mixing several varieties with combinations of fruit to produce "signature" breakfasts. A big bowl of Sag cereal combo, something interesting to read and familiar company makes for a pleasant start to the Sagittarius day.

While they love big special breakfast spreads (they love anything big and special that spreads), they are more inclined to be seduced on a regular basis by the breakfast sandwiches at fast food restaurants and convenience stores. Sagittarians are real fans of hot meat and cheese sandwiches on any occasion. If the truth be told, you're also likely to run across a few of these people on any morning at Denny's, enjoying the Grand Slam.

Even in the morning, these people are happiest when they're eating like horses.

What do you generally eat for breakfast?

Generally, nothing. Sometimes cereal and fresh fruit. Or a good bagel with cream cheese and tomato. There's too many things to do in the morning. I have to go work out. Maybe a banana.

What do you have if you're going to enjoy a special breakfast?

Steak and eggs. And a bowl of vanilla ice cream. I can eat ice cream anytime.

Sagittarius Breakfast Favorites

Juices: fresh orange
Fruits: fresh, in season
Cereal: whole grain and granola mixes; bran with raisins, strawberries and
    bananas
Sweet roll: fruit breads with sweet butter
Bread: flavored bagels with cream cheese
Egg dish: sausage and cheese omelet with biscuits and preserves
Other: French toast with real maple syrup; corned beef hash with poached
    eggs

Sagittarius Awayfood

It should already be clear that Sagittarians have few dining prejudices or pretenses. A list of their favorite restaurants will include at least one of every kind, from the plainest of the plastic to the highest of the *haute*. No other sign derives as much pleasure from the sheer diversity of dining establishments.

Sagittarians particularly love going out for exotic fare, although they sometimes experience then reject the likes of sea urchins, eels and miso soup. Conversely, they love a good steak or prime rib now and then. In all, their wide experience and lack of pose make them the best people to ask about "bests"—whether it's Italian food in Milan or chile in El Paso or seafood along the New Jersey shore.

Even with so many favorites, Sagittarians can speak quite eloquently when it comes to explaining how an establishment achieves stature with them. Much more than objective food quality and ambience, although these are both dear to the Sagittarius, the key issues are again ethical. Is this restaurant, the Sagittarian inevitably asks, meeting the philosophical and moral tenets of its *own* ambition?

Even more important to Sagittarians than having their own tastes satisfied is the indication that an establishment has a good attitude about whatever it is serving. Is the food offered, plated and served with pride? Does the cooking reflect intelligence, excitement and a familiarity with attractive flavor combinations? Is it appropriate to the price and the environment?

Likewise, service performance will be astutely judged. The Sagittarian simply asks "Is hospitality actually being rendered here?" Not unduly nervous about the finer points of tableside ballet—we are after all discussing good-humored people who regularly patronize hot dog stands—Sagittarians nevertheless expect to be sincerely served anywhere they dine.

Truly, what matters most to the Sagittarius is a restaurant's spirit, with the desirable keynotes being intelligence and generosity. The complimentary "our chef's been experimenting with this" appetizer or new wine sample scores vast goodwill points with Sagittarians. Conversely, they are more than capable of busting up a joint that tries to cut corners on "all-you-can-eat" night.

If escorting one of these beasts for a night on the town, it's worth remembering the sincere Sagittarian enjoyment of fine wines. With its complex yet subtle taste characteristics, its multiplicity of national and regional origins and its vast semi-historical/semi-hysterical lore, wine is a natural area for Sagittarian interest. And enough of the stuff makes them quite frisky.

What's important to you in the evaluation of a restaurant?

I read every word of the menu; it tells me where the chefs are at. Then I like to have something made special for me. I can really size the place up.

How do you decide to try a restaurant you've never been to before?

First, I read restaurant critiques. Second, I'll try anything new. Third, I'll ask a waiter at a place I already like. Fourth, I listen to friends' recommendations and do the opposite of what they say.

What new trends in the restaurant scene don't you like?

I hate the trend towards serving raw meat. God invented fire to keep us warm and light our way. The idea of passing a duck breast over a flame until slightly warm, and then charging double for it, is insane.

Romantic Menus for Sagittarius

To romance him:

Table: red and white checked tablecloth; Chianti candle
Appetizer: hot seafood antipasti
Bread: soft garlic breadsticks
Salad: iceberg wedge with anchovy-romano dressing
Entrée: herb-smoked filet; spaghetti carbonara; Szechuan vegetable medley
Wine: Amarone
Dessert: cannoli; sweet port

To romance her:

Table: bright personal statements (ceramics, natural materials, wild flow-
    ers)
Appetizer: fried cheese with homemade salsa
Bread: herb bread and sweet butter
Soup: chilled carrot with julienne dried fruit
Entrée: charred tuna filet; curried spinach fettucini with broccoli florets
Wine: Gewurztraminer
Dessert: green apple sorbet; homemade peanut butter cookies; Asti Spu-
    mante

Sagittarius Food Fantasy

The Sagittarius has elaborate fantasies about things like yachts, pin-up models and vast amounts of Hunan cuisine. Also about sultans' castles, pin-up models and HoHos made by Austrian pastry chefs. Also about tepees, pin-up models and maize.

But after searching far and wide for meaning and adventure, most Sagittarians eventually come to the conclusion that what matters most in life is appreciating the very real people with whom the search is shared—family, friends and soulmate strangers.

The Sagittarius would dearly enjoy taking all these people out to dinner. Everyone would board the Concorde and a long night would be spent travelling to the Sagittarian's favorite restaurants, everywhere in the world. There would, of course, also be great food and libation on the plane—probably a team of *garde mangers* and hors d'oeuvre chefs doing the cooking, and some thoroughly clever *sommeliers* dispensing fine wines and an assortment of good vermouths and diet sodas.

It would be a boundlessly happy, interesting and fulfilling time and, when it was over, no one would have to sleep alone.

Except it would probably go on forever.

What's your idea of a romantic meal?

> Once, when I was courting my wife, I picked her up from work in a chauffeured white Silver Cloud. We had champagne in plastic glasses and went to the Burger King Drive-Thru.

Appetizer Dip
submitted by Michael Reckling

2 cups sour cream
2 cups mayonnaise
2 packages frozen chopped spinach, thawed but not cooked
2 packages Knorr's vegetable soup mix

Combine all ingredients. Serve in hollowed-out sourdough loaf. Use as a dip for raw vegetables and the cut-out, cubed bread.

Squid Bake

submitted by Phil Allen

2 lbs. squid cleaned, skinned and sliced into half-inch rings
salt and pepper
4 cloves finely minced garlic
1/2 cup minced parsley
1/4 cup olive oil combined with juice of one lemon
Italian-style bread crumbs and grated parmesan cheese

Place a single layer of squid in a baking dish. Sprinkle with salt, pepper, garlic and parsley. Continue layering remainder of squid. Drizzle with lemon and oil and top with bread crumbs and cheese. Bake at 300° for 45 minutes. Serve with crusty bread to soak up the juices.

Lean Cuisine Orange Chicken

submitted by John W. Gamble

Salt to taste.

Potato Dill Soup

submitted by Amy Leonard

It's on page 60 of *The Vegetarian Epicure* by Ann Thomas.

Breakfast Cereal Combo

submitted by Denny Lewis

Mix equal parts of Fruit & Fibre, Raisin Bran, Raisin Grape Nuts, All-Bran and Mother's Oat Bran in a bowl. Add one package of sweetener and skim milk. If you're really hungry, slice a banana on top.

Artichokes Vieux Carré

submitted by Elin Jeffords

2 cups coarse, dry bread crumbs
1 cup parmesan cheese
1/2 cup finely chopped bitter Italian olives
5 finely chopped anchovies
4 finely chopped garlic cloves

Approximately 2 T. chopped parsley, basil, rosemary, etc.
coarse ground black pepper
olive oil to moisten slightly
4 large artichokes

Combine first eight ingredients in a bowl. Then, rinse artichokes, cut stem flat, trim leaf points off. Slam artichoke down point first on flat surface to spread leaves. Scrape choke out with tip of spoon.

Starting at the bottom, stuff a tad of bread crumb mixture down into base of each leaf (working over the bowl of crumbs makes it neater). Finish up with about a teaspoonful in the center of the heart. Repeat for each artichoke. Place in a glass baking dish, cover with plastic wrap and microwave on high seven minutes, turn dish half way and microwave five more minutes. Can be served hot or cold. If any crumb mixture is left it's great tossed with cooked vegetables, especially broccoli. (In fact, I often make it just for that.)

Shortbread

submitted by Hallie Donnelly

3 cups flour
3 cups sweet butter, softened
3/4 cup confectioner's sugar

Heat oven to 325°. Push the ingredients around until they're together. Roll out on sheet pan and prick with a fork. Bake for 40 minutes, until golden brown. Cut immediately after taking out of oven.

Shredded Apple Tart

submitted by June Robinson

3 green apples, shredded
lemon peel (optional)
orange juice and a small amount of lemon juice to make 1/4 cup
1-1/2 cups sugar
1-1/2 T. flour
2 eggs, well beaten

Mix everything together in a pre-baked deep dish pie shell. Bake at 450° for 10 minutes or 350° for 30 minutes.

Steamed Oreos

submitted by Louis Ekus

I love Oreos, but I don't like hard cookies. So in college I invented steamed Oreos. What you do is put a cooking screen over a pan filled with boiling water. Then you put the cookies on the screen and cover them with an aluminum foil tent. Cook for only about 30 to 40 seconds. If you steam them too long, you lose the middles. These should be enjoyed with a cold glass of milk while the cookies are still hot and the whole house is filled with Oreo smell. If there are leftovers, and there won't be, these keep well in sealed Tupperware containers in the refrigerator. This is the ultimate comfort food.

Some Sagittarian Food Personalities

Jaques Pepin, cookbook author and chef
Barry Wine, owner, Quilted Giraffe restaurant, New York City

Capricorn

December 22 to January 19

A fat kitchen, a lean will.

Benjamin Franklin (Capricorn), statesman
from *Poor Richard's Almanac*

*I was in Boston on a bus with my brother and I had a bag
of apples. I asked him:*
*"Do you remember what we used to have as appetiz-
ers on Friday night?"*
*"Grilled chicken livers," he answered correctly, and I
gave him an apple.*
*So then I asked him, "What did mom and dad have to
drink with the chicken livers?"*
*"Whiskey sours," he says, but at the same instant so
does this guy sitting in the seat behind us. So I gave
apples to both of them.*

Neil Cumsky (Capricorn), developer

Capricorns *can* be appreciated and, sometimes, even loved. Just because
they are generally hell-bent on world domination doesn't mean they are
without a sensitive and generous side. Even if wildly ambitious for themselves, they'll usually manage an apple for you too (if you earn it).

The Capricorn is a *careerist* in every sense of the word. No one has a more
thorough understanding of the concept of a life's work. Capricorns fret a great
deal over whether they are using their allotted time wisely, as well as over just
how much time has actually been allotted. Capricorns are determined, serious, rational, conservative and a bit sly.

No other sign creates, accepts and enforces the formal and informal rules
of society with more conviction, a characteristic that in the extreme borders
on snobbishness. However, Capricorns will bend and stretch the rules to the
limit, as they are often more than a little contemptuous of the nice guy who
finishes last. In personal relationships they need loyalty and second fiddling,
characteristics which they will reward with a sort of benevolent despotism.

Like other people Capricorns have to eat, but there may be no other sign whose collective attention is less captivated by the pleasures of the dinner table. The entire rigmarole of experiential dining seems small potatoes to the Capricorn, perhaps even harmful insofar as it consumes health and resources. Acknowledging the necessity of eating, Capricorns are inclined to ask: "But of what real *use* is food's *taste?*" When they find something they like, and if it's not too expensive, they will simply stick with it.

Not surprisingly, no one, not even a Cancer, has a better or fonder memory for the food of childhood. No matter how old they get, when the subject is good cooking Capricorns remain loyal to "mom." Outside the home, Capricorns are most interested in the social and business potential of dining situations, and they generally have a fair share of tableside graces if not enthusiasm for the food itself.

It is useful to note that Capricorns can be quite the private sensualists, which in part accounts for the atypically overweight Capricorns one encounters. However conservative and temperate their public consumption, most Capricorns have something chocolate hidden somewhere in the house. They're really not the sort to lick their fingers or pat their bellies in public but, in private, they'll enthusiastically lick your fingers and pat your tummy as well as their own.

On the whole, though, Capricorns lead socially proper lives. Their specific food choices are generally unadventurous, perhaps even boring to the more experientially-inclined signs. They will not miss a trick, though, when it comes to recognizing proper form, and they may surprise you when they order an interesting and absolutely appropriate wine or after-dinner drink.

If entertaining Capricorns, stick to the tried and true, watch your manners, don't muck up their dinners with culinary exotica and get your recipes from their moms. Don't expect a rave review (unless you *are* mom), but if everything cuts the mustard (a Capricorn favorite), you can be assured of a return portion of appreciation. Maybe even an apple.

Who is your favorite food authority?

I don't follow anyone.

What would be your idea of the perfect meal?

A red-sauce meal cooked by my mom with cacciatore, sausage and meatballs.

Ten Foods a Capricorn Needs to Survive on a Deserted Island

Bread • Chicken • Potatoes • Lettuce • Eggs
Ground beef • Cheese • Bananas • Coffee • Chocolate

What ten foods would you need to survive on a deserted island?

I could eat meat loaf every day.

I could eat chicken all the time.

Capricorn Island

On an isolated patch of beach front, the newly arrived Capricorns are inspecting their chosen survival food. Most have brought along staples, although a few have managed to outstaple the rest. One Capricorn has selected a pig, instead of choosing several pork products, and a chicken, so he would not have to waste a choice on eggs. He is busily chatting up another Capricorn who is showing off a string and safety pin rigged for fishing.

Up from the beach, most of the island looks like gentrified suburban countryside. In the populated areas the homes are large and solidly appointed, important-looking on their multi-acre parcels of land. Expensive European road cars are parked in the driveways, but nobody actually seems to like to drive. Hounds abound.

In Capricorn town, a major commercial and political center, there are a few outstanding grill restaurants, where important chefs artfully garnish their exquisitely simple creations, and where distinguished maître d's know the names and menu preferences of every customer. The island also boasts a special rustic old roadside place called "Mom's," that has been there for as long as anyone can remember and is famous for its home-style baked goods.

Visitors to Capricorn Island are amused by the quaint grocery store, which at first glance looks a bit like the place where Dobie Gillis' father used to work. A closer inspection, however, reveals consummate taste and craftsmanship in the store fixtures, including painstakingly finished ice chests, display cases and vegetable bins. The small selection of meats and produce is clearly of premium grade, although many of the prices are marked just a few cents off, as quality at a reduced price is a sales tactic Capricorns can't resist.

Many of the islanders themselves have never been to the grocery store. They prefer to have their orders delivered by industrious young lads on bicycles, whom they generally undertip. Larger orders come on Herbert T.'s panel truck.

Would you diet if you were stranded on a deserted island?

No, because I'd need strength to build a boat.

What would be your idea of the perfect meal?

A fried chicken dinner with mashed potatoes and gravy and frozen vegetables, cooked by my grandmother.

Capricorn Favorites

Vegetable: spinach, especially creamed; carrots
Fruit: banana
Starch: potato
Source of protein: chicken
Bread product: French or Italian, freshly baked
Dairy product: cheddar cheese, cottage cheese
Spice or herb: salt
Condiment: mustard
Ice cream flavor: chocolate chip
Pizza topping: extra cheese
Candy: solid chocolate

Cookie: Oreo
Sandwich: tuna with mayo
Soup: puree of vegetable with cream
Soft drink: Diet 7-Up, but none very popular
Beer: Miller Lite
Wine: Chardonnay
Liquor: vodka, Scotch
Liqueur: Amaretto, Grand Marnier
Comfort food: chocolate pudding
Celebration food: steak, grilled fish
Junk food: potato chips
Sexy food: whipped cream

What is your favorite comfort food?

Chocolate pudding. I remember as a child the magic moment when the pudding started to congeal in the pot.

A baked potato with butter, the way grandma would fix it for me.

What is your favorite dairy product?

Cottage cheese. You can put honey in it or jelly, which was my mother's way of doing it. I used to get this for a dessert sundae.

What is your favorite vegetable?

I like so many because I grew up on 'em.

Capricorn Diet and Health

The first people to diet were Capricorns, followed shortly by the Scorpios who wanted to get in on the pain. Unlike Scorpio, though, Capricorn is not into dieting for the anguish. It is simply the Capricorn's intention to stay healthy and present a good public image.

Actually, what the Capricorn considers normal intake is pretty much a diet to a lot of other signs. When a Capricorn diets, it's not all that distinguishable from starvation. For most Capricorns, it really is not that much of a hardship to reject the temptation of over-eating.

If a Capricorn goes in the other direction, however, there can be gluttonous devotion to the contents of the cupboard. Prompted by work stress or lack of success in romantic affairs, an unhappy Cappy is capable of living in the kitchen. Under these circumstances Capricorns will soothe themselves with high quality stuff, and local gourmet specialty stores will most certainly have reason to rejoice.

For most Capricorns, though, controlling food intake is simply a way of life. They exercise, take vitamins, reduce salt and cholesterol, and eat moderate amounts of animal protein. Their biggest indulgence is usually something like cottage cheese or yogurt with a little bit of imported jelly stirred in, although this sign definitely has its share of cigarette smokers (doesn't show around the hips).

It's worth knowing that Capricorns feel betrayed by their bodies when sickness sets in, and they can be very difficult about being even a little bit ill. They don't want to die before they discover the meaning of life. They want their mommy.

Chocolate pudding and tiny marshmallows will sometimes help.

Do you ever diet? How?

Constantly. I starve myself.

Would you diet on a deserted island?

What for? Nobody would see me.

Do you have any personal nutritional habits or beliefs?

My body craves what it needs.

Ten More Foods Most Capricorns Like a Whole Lot

Cottage cheese • Crackers • Broccoli • Roast pork • Yogurt • Steak
Mayonnaise • Grilled fish • Orange juice • Red-flavored infant food

Things You Should Not Feed a Capricorn

Very smelly foods
Very slimy foods

What are some foods or flavors that turn you off?

Caviar. I detest it. It tastes like bile.

Pizza. I eat it to be polite.

Capricorn Homefood

Most Capricorns are passionately interested in the past. They love to learn about the lives of the famous and the infamous, to see what pointed them down the roads of success and failure. To a Capricorn, any history amounts to exceedingly useful advice.

Add to this the way a Capricorn feels about mom. Mom is the first teacher and the forgiving nurturer. Her beliefs establish the value grid of the Capricorn soul. She is the foundation from which all future striving proceeds and the archetypal evaluator by whom success is truly measured.

Rare, then, is the Capricorn who doesn't have vivid and adoring memories of the food served by mom, and who doesn't still have some affinity for such nursery food as bananas, cooked carrots, cottage cheese and pudding. Even if mom was an admittedly terrible cook, there is still a remembered taste, maybe of a tough burned little pork chop, that still brings a tear to the eye. If mom was a good cook you may never hear the end of it, and you will never garner as much culinary praise.

Capricorn husbands are the ones who beg their wives to go to mom and learn how to cook. One successful Capricorn restaurateur has his mother's phone number posted in each of his six restaurant kitchens. Heaven help his cooks if the tomato sauce and key lime pie vary from the sacred originals.

Capricorn women almost invariably cook like their mothers. If mom was either a solid basic home cook or a very confident social chef, the talent is inherited. Interestingly, Capricorns whose mothers were bad cooks usually hate to cook, feeling they have no talent for it and are damned if they will publicly fail at anything.

In most cases Capricorns will not be too food-fussy at home, provided daily food is kept simple and family holidays are remembered with ceremonial fare. Their refrigerators should be stocked with cheddar and mustard, and a box of Saltines should be handy at all times.

Capricorns like to nibble while plotting about becoming big cheeses.

Is your mother a good cook?

Oh yes. Has anyone answered no?

Do you like to cook?

No, I hate it. I'm not any good at it.

Yes, things I know.

Why do you like to cook?

I like a sense of working hard before I eat.

What's the most interesting thing in your refrigerator?

Six jars of my mother's tomato sauce.

Capricorn Breakfast

On a weekday, Capricorns are all business about breakfast. While dressing for the office, they drink their first cup of coffee. When dressed, they take their vitamins with orange juice and, if time has been budgeted, linger over a second cup of coffee with some toast and a serious newspaper.

They like having their families around in the morning, as this tends to keep them a little less hyper than when they are alone. The solitary Capricorn frequently starts working at breakfast with calendars, to-do-lists, and general outlines for world conquest. They try to avoid foods that are sticky on a Day-Timer, but they do have a weakness for yogurt, all soft fruits and any form of cheese.

On the weekends, especially Sunday morning, the Capricorn is a much easier beast to bear. Even a Capricorn knows it's downright traditional to relax, read the paper and have a nice big breakfast on Sunday morning. Knowing there is full social sanction for such behavior, the Capricorn is generally pleasant and attentive company.

Why, they'll even find some time to call mom. Just have breakfast on the table before they do.

Do you like to eat breakfast?

No, probably because my mother forced it on me as a child.

Capricorn Breakfast Favorites

Juices: orange, grapefruit
Fruits: bananas, berries, prunes
Cereals: granola, Raisin Bran
Sweet rolls: cheese Danish
Bread: toasted sourdough or rye
Egg dish: cheese omelet
Other: buckwheat pancakes with real maple syrup

Capricorn Awayfood

Capricorns love to be in control of situations, so there are elements of dining out that can lead to trouble. It usually starts with a waiter who somehow offends the Capricorn. It is easy for service people to offend a Capricorn who is, after all, a bit of a snob.

An insult may come in the form of perceived aloofness. Or too much familiarity. Or a water glass is left empty, or an ashtray full, for more than thirty seconds.

It's not hard to do it. And if it happens, the meal will be ruined for everyone—for the Capricorn's company, who will have to listen to the failure of the place to measure up; for the waiter, who has every right to fear the size of his forthcoming tip; and, of course, for the Capricorn, who will have control but who will also have alienated everybody.

Another one of the Capricorn's worries about favorite restaurants is that something will be different in the food this trip. A seasoning will have been adjusted or a garnish changed. This the Capricorn can treat as a plot against history.

The other side of the coin is that Capricorns are incredibly loyal to establishments that are consistent in quality. While it sometimes appears that they like the "in" spots, it is more appropriately said that they like the "good" spots. And this is not so much a function of the moment as it is of the restaurant management's *long-term* organization, environmental sensitivity, food and service performance, and general business acumen.

So don't be offended if Capricorn doesn't heed your restaurant recommendation. You must be a very trusted source, whose taste has been personally evaluated by the Capricorn, before you can be trusted for this kind of information. And even then the Capricorn will not be convinced unless your story can be backed up.

If you're really trying to impress a Capricorn, go somewhere a maître d' knows your name. Better yet, call ahead and tell the maître d' the Capricorn's name. Their delight at a formal yet familiar personal greeting will be orgasmic (but restrained).

If you want to relax with a Capricorn, take them to a place that has really good home-style cooking (the Capricorn's home style) or prepare a meal at home yourself. Capricorns love familiar and nostalgic foods presented with pride and sincerity. But never forget, nobody will ever cook as well as mom.

What gets you to try a restaurant you've never been to before?

A recommendation from a trusted source, but I don't really trust others' opinions.

What's important to you in the evaluation of a restaurant?

The first person I meet. If they're snotty or just not pleasant, I feel totally unwelcome.

What's your favorite romantic restaurant?

It's a local place. When I go there, food is the last thing on my mind. In fact, the food is lousy.

What's your favorite hotel restaurant?

I never had a decent meal in a hotel in my life.

What new trends on the restaurant scene do you like?

I like the trend to light spa cuisine, and I also like the nostalgia trend.

Romantic Menus for Capricorn

To romance him:

Table: French bread and butter
Appetizer: cheese and crackers
Soup: cream of tomato
Entrée: grilled chicken; home-fried potatoes; creamed spinach
Wine: Chardonnay
Dessert: banana cream pie and coffee

To romance her:

Table: bread sticks
Appetizer: country paté with imported mustard *or* tossed salad with goat
    cheese and mustard dressing
Soup: seafood bisque
Entrée: charcoal-broiled filet; baked potato with sour cream
Wine: Cabernet Sauvignon
Dessert: chocolate mousse with raspberry sauce; coffee

What would be your idea of the perfect meal?

> I'd be waited on hand and foot by waiters and waitresses who
> wouldn't do a bloody thing except what I told them to do.

Capricorn Food Fantasy

His:

He has just concluded a tremendously advantageous business deal, slaughtering a tough business opponent in the process. Now he's meeting the vanquished foe's beautiful wife, who has slipped some serious hints during the course of her husband's negotiations. He's got to get her out of the restaurant quickly, though, as there's no telling who they might run into.

He puts forth the business of *l'amour* and she accepts the terms. He asks if she is really hungry and she gets the point. He summons the waiter.

"Francisco, tell my mother that we had to leave. Business emergency. I'll be back for dinner."

He takes her back to his office and handcuffs her to the couch.

Later that night he returns to his mother's restaurant. With the extra notice, she has had time to personally whip up some of his favorite boyhood specialties. Seeing that he is alone, she joins him at the table. And while he eats, she tells him what a proud mom she is.

Hers:

It is a few moments past sundown. In the dining room of a beautiful old mountain lodge, she sits with her exquisitely handsome and successful husband. Theirs was a relationship late in coming to fruition, but there is now about them a sense of timelessness, an enduring love.

In the distance, outside the restaurant's picture window, the mountains are turning blue. He reaches to touch her hand and candlelight dances off their expensive jewelry. Underneath the table, he uses his other hand discreetly to massage her knee.

As one waiter clears the empty crystal supreme dishes, a second refreshes the wine glasses. A third charmingly recommends the broiled swordfish and her husband agrees also to share a *petit* filet mignon. Soon it is quiet again, as darkness swallows the mountains and the candle illumination lingers.

After something chocolate, with lots of fresh raspberries and whipped cream, she leaves the dining room on her husband's arm. In their room, they inhale some Amaretto while sipping the night air. On a bear rug, in front of a fireplace, their lovemaking is straightforward, intense and sincere.

In the morning, over mimosas and freshly baked croissants, he mentions that he has purchased her the lodge as a gift.

What would be your idea of the perfect meal?

I would eat it with someone who adored me and made me feel like a million bucks.

I don't want my son around unless he grows up.

Chicken and Noodles

submitted by Phyllis Gardner
(I do it the way my mom does it, with the whole chicken.)

2 cans white chicken chunks
1/2 stick butter
small onion, chopped
a couple of celery sticks, also chopped

Put in pressure cooker with two bags of shell noodles and salt and pepper. Fill pressure cooker up with water to cover noodles. After it starts jiggling cook for 5 minutes at the highest pressure. Voilà!

Homemade Ketchup

submitted by Charles Irvine
(My mom showed me how to make this.)

1 number 10 can of tomatoes
salt and pepper
onion
green pepper
brown sugar
a dash of vinegar

Remove the seeds and mash the tomatoes and cook down with the other ingredients. This is a great topping for navy beans. It's chunky like chow chow.

Glazed Ham with Dijon Mustard

submitted by Sally Brown

You get it out of the first Julie Rosso *Silver Palate Cookbook.*

Pork Roast

submitted by Donna Whitley

1 pork roast
potatoes, peeled and chopped
green chiles, diced
onions, yellow
lots of onion salt, garlic salt, salt and pepper

Cook it in a pressure cooker until it's so well done that it falls apart. Take the juice out and thicken with cornstarch. It looks like stew.

Smoky Turkey

submitted by Howard Solganik

2 handfuls wood chips
1 whole turkey breast, 6 to 8 pounds
salt (optional)

Soak the chips in water for at least 20 minutes. With the vents open on the grill, build a fire for the indirect method of cooking. That means to arrange the coals around a drip pan about the size of the turkey. When the coals are covered with a gray ash, add the soaked chips to the charcoal. Sprinkle turkey with salt if desired and place on the grill, bone side down. Put the cover on the grill and cook the turkey 11 to 13 minutes per pound.

Greatest Stuffing in the World

submitted by Judy Shoen
(I have to have this on Thanksgiving.)

3 cups chopped onions
2 cups chopped celery with leaves
1-1/2 cups butter
1-1/2 lbs. country pork sausage from the butcher
1 cup mushrooms, coarsely chopped
8 cups Pepperidge Farm seasoned stuffing
16 oz. chestnuts, crumbled, from a jar
2 cups chopped apricots
2 cups raisins, mixed brown and gold
1-1/2 to 2 cups pine nuts
3 eggs
2 cups rich chicken stock
2 green apples, chopped
1/4 cup wine
1 t. nutmeg
2 t. sage
1 t. rosemary
1 t. fresh pepper

Sauté onion and celery in butter until tender. In a separate skillet, cook sausage and mushrooms; drain fat. Combine vegetables, sausage and mushrooms. Add bread crumbs. Combine with everything. Moisten with chicken stock. Makes approximately 20 cups.

Bread Pudding

submitted by VaLinda Parsons
(This is my mother's)

4 cups day-old bread cubes
3 cups milk
3 eggs
1/3 cup sugar

1 t. vanilla extract
1/2 cup raisins
cinnamon and nutmeg, to taste

Combine all ingredients except spices and pour into greased 1-1/2 quart casserole. Bake for about 40 minutes at 350°. Sprinkle with spices before or after baking. Good served with cream, whipped cream or ice cream over it while pudding is still warm.

Poppy Seed Cake

submitted by Neil Cumsky

1/2 cup butter
3/4 cup sugar
2 large eggs
1/2 cup sour cream
1/3 cup poppy seeds
1/4 cup orange juice

1 T. grated orange peel
1 t. vanilla
1-1/2 cups all-purpose flour
1/2 t. baking powder
1/4 t. soda
a pinch of salt

Cream butter and sugar until light and fluffy; beat in eggs one at a time. Add sour cream, poppy seeds, orange peel and vanilla. Stir in flour, baking powder, soda and salt; mix well. Pour batter into floured 1-quart ring mold. Bake at 350° for 45 minutes; let cool completely; dust with powdered sugar; sprinkle with poppy seeds.

Some Capricorn Food Personalities

Pierre Franey, chef and cookbook author
Danny Kaye, actor and epicurean

Aquarius

January 20 to February 18

Ah, but porcupine pie, porcupine pie, porcupine pie
It weaves its way through my dreams.
And I do believe I'm gonna try some
And leave some room for dessert
Chicken ripple ice cream.

> Neil Diamond (Aquarius), songwriter
> from the album *Hot August Nights*

Ashford, Conn. *Paul Newman fulfilled another dream Wednesday, breaking ground on a 300-acre camp here for children who are seriously and terminally ill.*

"From salad dressings all blessings flow," said the 61-year-old actor [Aquarian], whose Newman's Own food company, which he founded with A.E. Hotchner, has raised $9 million for charities. Profits from his dressings, spaghetti sauce and popcorn sales will pay for half of the $8 million camp.

> *USA Today*, Dec. 11, 1986

What kind of food does an Aquarian like? That's a little like asking what kind of food the Jabberwock likes. Even if you were told, would you really know?

It is almost impossible to anticipate an Aquarius. Always thinking, compelled to probe, analyze, experiment, discover and reveal, Aquarius is midwife to the omnipresent becoming omnifuture. To appreciate an Aquarius is to appreciate the full breadth of the possibilities of perception.

The trouble a lot of other signs have with an Aquarius is that it is sometimes just too damn hard to know what the hell an Aquarius is talking about. Aquarian perception works on a playing field with incredibly wide boundary markers. Aquarians zoomthink laterally, slicing deftly through billions of brain cells, before planting themselves and throwing the bomb to the mouth upfield.

Perhaps it helps to think of a computer graphics program. Aquarians can rotate designs, words and concepts in their minds, rapidly changing, combin-

153

ing and deleting elements, to get a good look at just about anything from a myriad of mind perspectives. They are engineers of thought.

When it comes to any remotely conceivable matter in the universe, including food, Aquarians will generally play it one of two ways. Either the new matter will barely register on the field of consciousness because the Aquarian is so deeply absorbed in something else. Or endless wonders of the universe will be revealed in a Triscuit.

In truth (the Aquarian motto), Aquarians sometimes seem to be food fetishists. They will eat the same food, or category of food, almost exclusively for months on end. In this way they really get to know peanut butter and snack crackers, for example, while they avoid crowding their taste brain cells with a lot of superfluous flavor input.

Aquarians who become professionally interested in a broader spectrum of food experience often become the trendsetters in the dining field. Aquarians are the restaurateurs who invent and introduce new concepts and menu items to the public. Aquarians are the restaurant market analysts who foresee the coming of new tastes and styles.

Most astrologers know Aquarius as the sign of the humanitarian, and Aquarians always seem to have a wide circle of friends and group involvements. Subsequently, it turns out that many of an Aquarian's favorite foods are those consumed at happy public gatherings (or, as in the case of Aquarian Paul Newman, are those same foods mass produced and sold for the benefit of less fortunate members of society). Aquarians usually love pizza, birthday cake, cheap champagne, popcorn—the *table d'hôte* of any amusement park, baseball stadium or really friendly party.

Literally and metaphorically, Aquarians like to pierce dry casings and discover moist airiness within. Favorite foods include grapes and blueberries, juicy sausages, lobster (although Aquarians are sincerely troubled by the pain potential of the boiling water), soft-shelled crabs and tacos, and just about anything hidden in pastry or pasta. They love airy foods like soufflé and mousse, and especially carbonated beverages.

The best thing about catering to Aquarians is that they are extremely versatile and adaptable guests, and are more than disposed to trying something different. The only suggestion here is that you check with them before actually serving porcupine pie. Quite a few Aquarians are humanely disposed towards vegetarianism (although they will still applaud your originality in suggesting the dish).

Do you like to cook?

Yes, I love to feed other people.

What's your favorite cookbook?

Gala Dinners by Salvador Dali.

Ten Foods an Aquarius Needs to Survive on a Deserted Island

Chicken • Milk • Eggs • Tomato sauce • Idaho potatoes
A fruit basket • Pasta • Carbonated water • Peanut butter
Chocolate chip cookies

What ten foods would you need to survive on a deserted island?

Yogurt, milk, eggs—hey, I'm from Wisconsin, what do you want?

Aquarius Island

Aquarians are attuned to the flow and ebb of life. They themselves are ease and intensity, happy and sad, up and down, fast and slow, forward and back, round and round, although not necessarily in that order. Much of Aquarius Island is simply a vast empty expanse (the "vex") where the inhabitants can go off by themselves, stand on their heads and contemplate truth and posture.

Aquarians arrive at the vex via the island's public transportation system, electronic rocket trains on elevated roller coaster tracks. Snacks are served on board, so the loop-de-loops have been centrifugally engineered to prevent upside down drinks from spilling. Sometimes the system is run backwards, but the centrifugal principle still holds.

Most public activity takes place in an environment that would feel homey to the Jetsons. Everywhere people are landing on and living in space pads. For cooking, everyone has a futuristic device in their pad which enables prepared food to be presented at the tug of a few toggles, or there is at least a microwave oven.

Public entertainment centers abound in Aquarius City, including sports complexes, theaters, hands-on museums, shopping malls, boardwalks, theme parks and zoos with talking animals. These are all among the islanders' favorite places to eat. Throughout the many public areas are food kiosks and carts, each with its own street-cooked specialty and character-actor proprietor.

The dining pride of Aquarius Island sits atop the tallest space pad. A landmark clear-domed restaurant serves innovative fine food and, even better, presents spectacular islandscapes and premier people-watching. After dinner the dome is darkened and, with the aid of advanced holographic projections of cosmos and Cuisinarts, the restaurant's chef-owner gives stirring talks on cooking and astrology.

What is your favorite fast food item?

Big Mac with real French mayonnaise-based super sauce with fresh tarragon, like when they first opened.

Aquarius Favorites

Vegetable: sweet corn
Fruit: all
Starch: pasta
Source of protein: chicken
Bread product: fruit muffins
Dairy product: milk
Spice or herb: garlic, cinnamon
Condiment: Dijon mustard (highly whipped, like Grey Poupon)
Ice cream flavor: strawberry, cherry vanilla
Pizza topping: mushrooms
Candy: jelly beans
Cookie: bakery chocolate chip

Sandwich: turkey, Swiss, avocado and sprouts on whole wheat
Soup: hot and sour with noodles, mushrooms and chicken
Soft drink: iced tea
Beer: Coors Light
Wine: sparkling
Liquor: gin and tonic
Liqueur: Frangelica
Comfort food: pizza
Celebration food: bakery cake
Junk food: grocery store cookies
Sexy food: strawberries with whipped cream

What is your favorite spice?

Tarragon. I know it's not a spice but it tastes like one.

What is your favorite candy?

Kit Kat. Those little wafers get to me.

What is your favorite fruit?

Magonets. They come from Indonesia. I think they do.

What is a sexy food?

Very ripe pears or figs.

Chocolate. It depends on the mold.

An ice cream cone.

Flavored body oils.

Creole barbecued shrimp.

Aquarius Diet and Health

Aquarians are experimenters and mental wanderers, so their dietary habits are not that consistent. Many Aquarians will simply answer "none," if questioned as to dietary beliefs and practices. But they will still have opinions, just like everyone else.

Many Aquarians feel closely bonded to their animal brethren, and the sign has a lot of vegetarians. It is the rare Aquarian, in any circumstance, who will eat a lot of red meat, although it is sometimes appreciated as a variety item. Generally, the Aquarian is much more into fluids, fruits, vegetables, carbohydrates and herbal stimulants than protein.

Aquarians can be very flabby and illness-prone or very lean and well-conditioned. Aquarians often experience both these extremes in their lifetimes, although they sometimes discover that they can be flabby and health-prone or very lean and sickly. They do not pretend that such things can't happen because to Aquarians they do.

Aquarians usually have the inner resolve to diet when absolutely necessary, but they are not the kind of people to subscribe to other people's dietary theories. There will usually be at least one quirk in a diet, maybe a "magical" food that keys a personal metabolic response.

Although they are sometimes sedentary through long periods of mental activity, they are usually strong believers in the benefits of exercise. Aquarian favorites include lap swimming, tennis and skiing—anything associated with strong rhythmic variations, a lot of intense back and forth and a club with a friendly bar.

Do you have any personal nutritional habits or beliefs?

Yeah, I try not to eat too much junk.

Do you ever diet?

Never. I am philosophically opposed towards all forms of self-restraint.

Yes. A positive self-concept brings as much pleasure as good food.

Does that include your past life?

Ten More Foods Most Aquarians Like a Whole Lot

Flour • Oil • Vinegar • Rice • Onions • Shrimp
Spinach • Mushrooms • Popcorn • Pizza

Things You Should Not Feed an Aquarius

A lot of red meat
A lot of organ meats
Whole anchovies

What are some foods or flavors that turn you off?

Caramel. It's too sweet. It's over the borderline.

Beets, mincemeat and ouzo.

Aquarius Homefood

Aquarians are not typically devoted to the details of their personal spaces. They generally get along fine with modest living quarters, preferably on the modern or natural side. They do require some personal space, however, and they appreciate their homes as studies, entertainment centers and safe harbors.

Most Aquarians do like to cook, at least sometimes, when the food preparation can be spontaneous, creative and done for an appreciative audience. They can exhibit a real flair for people-pleasing gastronomy under these circumstances, coming up with all sorts of wonderful dishes and wondrous explanations. Their favorite cooking technique is sauté/stir-fry, due to its limitless variety of flavor and ingredient combinations and its energy efficiency.

Mostly, though, the Aquarian life is the snacking life. These people will "graze" both inside and outside the home, and it is always possible to find them exploring or gazing dreamily into an open cupboard. Actually, the correct term for the way Aquarians eat might be "crazing."

There are always idiosyncrasies with Aquarius. Their refrigerators are like the old wedding superstition, containing something old (vegetables), something new (a statue of Godzilla), something borrowed (a flashlight) and something blue (the vegetables). Aquarians do have a strong propensity for overbuying fruits and vegetables, perhaps because of some perverse scientific fascination with the processes of dehydration and decay (perverse, that is, until they discover penicillin).

They are not particularly sentimental, but they do look forward to the parties that holidays bring. Unlike Capricorn, they are very honest about assessing maternal culinary talent and are rarely over-fond. They usually have more enthusiastic recollections of prepared food brought into the home or of family dining in restaurants.

Do you like to cook? Why?

I love to cook. It's something that everyone appreciates.

Is your mother a good cook?

No. But don't tell her.

What was your mother's best dish?

Potato salad. Her one masterpiece.

What's your favorite kitchen appliance?

A guinea pig cage with occupant.

What's the most interesting thing in your refrigerator?

A statue of Godzilla.

Aquarius Breakfast

Many Aquarians are self-employed or hold odd-hour jobs, and there is a tendency for their days not to be nine-to-five-ish. Even if on a normal clock cycle, the Aquarian is liable to reach for last night's cold pizza or left-over popcorn in the morning, feeling no compunction to subscribe to prevailing breakfast theory. It's not that they don't like breakfast foods, but who says a chicken prefers that you eat its eggs in the morning?

There is some particular enjoyment of cereal, milk and fruit. Picture someone in their bed clothes at the kitchen table, hunched over a bowl intensely studying the cereal box. A funny-looking drinking mug stands to one side of the bowl, while the other side plays host to the eager milk-lapping of the Aquarian's pet kitty. Aquarians will tell you that they consume cereal for health reasons, but it's really because of cereal boxes and pet cats.

Aquarians do not really care who is around in the morning, as long as they have no behavioral expectations of the Aquarian. They're not usually the early bird sort, unless they're sneaking out before dawn to play golf. The typical Aquarian needs a little time to remember who and where they are.

If they are alone and feel the need for company, they will invest the inanimate objects in their surroundings with personality. Aquarians like to ask their clothes if they feel like being worn that day. Sometimes they will turn on the TV and talk to Willard Scott.

Aquarians *are* snap, crackle and pop.

What is your favorite breakfast food?

I consider hash brown potatoes and eggs a total nightmare.

Scrambled eggs and hash browns.

Pepsi.

Do you like breakfast?

I don't eat it. Dick doesn't eat it either. But if people call us long distance on the telephone we call them back. We have a new espresso machine but it is too hard to work in the morning.

Aquarius Breakfast Favorites

Juices: cranapple, papaya
Fruits: melons, berries
Cereals: all
Sweet rolls: cinnamon buns
Breads: bagels
Egg dish: to order with bacon, hash browns and fruit garnish
Other: bacon waffles with blueberry compote

Aquarius Awayfood

Are they OK to take out in public? Must the bizarre be always just within their reach? Are they dangerous?

Aquarians can be great comrades in almost any experience, but there are inevitably a few tics. Stubbornness about personal habits, moodiness in the face of pleasure, extremism in the defense of everything, an electric temper; these are a few of their favorite things. No other signs shows a stronger tendency towards public displays of self-righteousness (the Leo's knack is self-interest), or is as frequently deserving of a swift kick for the behavior.

With this regrettable trait noted, it can be truthfully said that no sign more enjoys going out with friends to eat and have a good time. Aquarians are in heaven—they are particularly fond of restaurants in high open places—if they can simply be with interesting people and look at interesting sights. Aquarians can be happy at a fast food mall, or a sports pub, or a neighborhood Italian restaurant provided that there is something interesting to look at and people are enthusiastically getting along.

Of course, it might be wise for a potential host to pre-determine if an Aquarian guest is one who happens to be into food and dining. This sign can expertly analyze anything to which the mind is set, and more than one unwitting escort has had a fond food intention dashed by a sincere Aquarian evaluation. The flaw most often noted is imitative trendiness, which the trend-setting Aquarius sees as manipulative and boring.

Aquarians can cut as deftly with a remark as with a knife, they are prone to unusual behavior and they frequently drift away into their own wide realms of inner observation. Still, you'd never call their company dull. And they always seem to get along great with the service staff and the people at the next table.

Best of all, they really can recognize when it is absolutely necessary to act responsibly, and they have very sincere smiles.

What is your favorite fast food chain?

It doesn't exist. But if it did I'd order one of their ethereal seafood pastas.

What new trends in the restaurant scene do you like? Are there any that you don't like?

I like the reliability of chain restaurants. I don't like that chain restaurants are forcing the independent guys out of business.

Romantic Menus for Aquarius

To romance him:

Table: something to play with (cards, a top, a harmonica)
Appetizer: stuffed mushrooms
Soup: corn, clam, potato and bacon chowder
Entrée: barbecued turkey or pork sandwich on grilled sourdough; dill
   pickle; corn chips
Beverage: choice of light beer, carbonated water or coffee
Dessert: ice cream novelty (chicken ripple?)

To romance her:

Table: garlic bread
Appetizer: fresh pasta tossed with fresh vegetables, fresh lobster meat and
    fresh cream
Soup: unnecessary
Entrée: spinach salad with hot bacon dressing *or* Caesar salad
Wine: Blush Zinfandel
Dessert: Frangelica soufflé with fresh berry sauce; coffee; after-dinner
    mints

Aquarius Food Fantasy

What sort of food fantasy does an Aquarian have? That's a little like asking
what sort of fantasy the Jabberwock has. Even if you were told, would you
really know?

These people live such intense and free-ranging mental lives that nothing
conceivable is foreign to their imaginations. An Aquarian food fantasy might
involve a buffet in outer space; or a picnic with Snow White, replete with
dwarves and poison apples; or conversation with the Apostles at the Last
Supper; or a flavored-oil demo involving TV personalities; or a pajama brunch
at the beach with talking dolphins—or anything at all. As one Aquarian so
aptly responded when asked for a food fantasy:

"I can't answer that. My life is fantasy."

It may be ultimately true for both the sons and daughters of Aquarius,
and there is a marked androgynous quality to the Aquarian temperament,
that the real fantasy is participation in the mundane. Sitting in an attractive
room with an attractive view, enjoying attractive food with attractive company—and having absolutely nothing out of the ordinary happen to jar a
simple pleasant mood—to Aquarius, this happens only in dreams. Sweet
dreams, Aquarius.

Who is your favorite luncheon companion?

Diet 7-Up.

What would be your idea of the perfect meal?

It would be in a beach house on the coast in Big Sur, California.
We'd have barbecue chicken, hamburgers, ribs, salads, rolls, appe-
tizers, beer and wine. I'd invite Tom, Billie, Rita, Mel, Chuck, Leslie,
Sonny, Dana, Dave, Janice, Glenn, Caryn and Dick.

Italian Meat Loaf

submitted by Jan Buckingham

1 cup soft bread crumbs (preferably French or Italian bread)
1/2 cup milk
1 package (10 oz.) frozen chopped spinach, thawed
1 lb. veal, finely ground
1 lb. lean beef, ground
1/2 lb. sweet Italian sausage, removed from casing and chopped or
    crumbled
1/2 cup onion, finely minced
2 eggs, well beaten
1 T. salt
1/2 t. dried basil
1/2 t. dried thyme
1/2 t. ground nutmeg
1/2 cup parmesan cheese (fresh, if possible), grated or shredded
1/2 cup pine nuts (pignola) or shelled green pistachio nuts
1 cup peas, fresh or frozen (thawed)
garlic

Preheat oven to 350°. Soak the bread crumbs in milk for 10 minutes. Drain the thawed spinach well and squeeze out any excess moisture. Squeeze the milk from the crumbs. In a bowl, combine the bread crumbs, spinach and meat with the onion, eggs, salt, herbs and cheese. Mix lightly with hands or a large wooden spoon until ingredients are just blended. Fold in the nuts and peas.

Gently pat the meat mixture into 2 long, thick loaves, about 10" long. (Do not pack too tightly, as this tends to make a tough loaf.) Score the top lightly. Place in a large baking pan and bake for 1-1/2 hours, basting frequently with pan juices. If possible, turn the meat over during the final 15 minutes of baking. Allow to cool in pan, brushing occasionally with pan juices. Place each loaf on a piece of foil large enough to wrap. Cut each loaf into 12-14 slices. Wrap and refrigerate. (One loaf can be frozen for later use.) Serves sixteen to twenty.

Spaghetti Squash Romano

submitted by Sandy Thymore

1 large spaghetti squash
2-3 garlic cloves or prepared minced
   garlic
1/4 cup romano-parmesan cheese

1/2 t. oregano
1/2 t. salt
1/4 cup olive oil
1/2 lb spaghetti, cooked

Split large spaghetti squash in half lengthwise and scoop out seeds and stringy material. Place cut side down in baking pan with 2" water and bake at 350° until fork tender, approximately 20 to 25 minutes. Cool. With a fork scoop out strands until all are out of shell. In sauté pan heat olive oil and garlic, being careful not to burn. Add squash, oregano and salt, and cook very slowly. Mix this with spaghetti (or other favorite pasta), toss with cheese. Place in serving dish and decorate with pimiento and baby peas for color. Approximately four servings.

Vintage Seafood Tarragon

submitted by Olwen Claiborne

1/2 cup bay scallops
1/2 cup shrimp, shelled, deveined
1-2 cloves garlic (to taste)
2 T. butter
1/4 cup chicken bouillon
1 handful snow peas, stringed
1 handful mushrooms, wiped and
   sliced

minced onion to taste
tarragon to taste
Chablis to taste
8 oz. tri-colored linguine or
   fettucine, cooked
salt and pepper to taste
1 oz. cream cheese

Brown garlic in butter. Sauté onions until golden, remove and set aside. Sauté mushrooms until just tender, remove and set aside. Add snow peas, stir until just tender, remove and set aside. Add bouillon, Chablis, tarragon, salt and pepper to pan, heat. Add scallops and shrimp, cook until firm, remove and set aside. Introduce cream cheese to juices and bouillon mixture, simmer until melted and sauce thickens slightly. Correct seasoning. Place all vegetables and seafood back in pan, stir until food is coated and heated. Serve in two heated soup plates over cooked pasta. Garnish with snow peas and mushroom slices. Serves two.

Peanut Butter Chocolate-Chip Sandwich

submitted by Gayle Payne

2 slices whole wheat bread
2 T. peanut butter
2 T. semi-sweet chocolate chips

Variations: add apple slices (pippin or other tart variety), or use crackers topped with peanut butter and *mini* semi-sweet chocolate chips

Pudding Pizza

submitted by Steven Mark Weiss

Crust:
1 17 oz. package Pillsbury sugar cookie dough
non-stick cooking spray as required
Topping:
1 small box (4 serving) Jell-O French vanilla instant pudding
1-1/4 cups cold milk
1 cup thawed Cool Whip
approx. 2 cups fresh fruit (sliced bananas, halved grapes, sliced straw-
    berries, blueberries, pineapple chunks)
1/3 cup miniature marshmallows
1/3 cup chocolate chips
1/3 cup chopped pecans
1/3 cup shredded coconut

Crust: cut cookie dough as for cookies, in 1/4-inch slices. Place on lightly sprayed 12" pizza pan and press out evenly into bottom and sides to form a solid crust. Bake at 350° for approx. 15 minutes, until golden brown. Cool before adding topping.

Topping: prepare pudding mix as directed on package for pudding, reducing milk to 1-1/4 cups. Let stand 5 minutes, then fold in Cool Whip. Shortly before serving, spread pudding mixture evenly over the crust. Do your own thing with the fruits, marshmallows, chips, pecan and coconut. Cut with a pizza wheel for maximum effect.

How About a Favorite Menu Instead?

submitted by Penny Gardner

Chicken, apples, curry and other spices slowly cooked in a clay cooking pot
Twice-baked potatoes with parmesan cheese
Mushrooms stuffed with crab and cream cheese
Cranberries in strawberry Jell-O with whipped topping
Lemon meringue pie
Sparkling Burgundy

Some Aquarius Food Personalities

Dinah Shore, entertainer, cookbook author, food spokesperson
Burt Reynolds, actor and dinner theater owner
Sonny Bono, singer and restaurateur
Michael McCarthy, owner, Michael's, Santa Monica, California

Pisces

February 19 to March 20

Spiritual and emotional hungers which induce psychosomatic illnesses are undoubtedly as widespread as are vitamin and mineral hungers, and therefore faulty nutrition is by no means the only cause of illness.

Adelle Davis (Pisces), nutritionist
from *Let's Cook It Right*

I love to eat. I love to eat. It's important, but I'm not going to go crazy.

Marilyn Hawkes (Pisces), wife and mother and friend

Steamed artichokes come to mind. Vapor-dappled hues of dusky olive and deep sea-green, bishop-crown fingers folded in upon themselves in the suggestion of prayer, each congregation concealing in its depth the mystery of a rich secret heart. Unarguably natural, artichokes seem more representational than real, works of spirit and art rather than randomly evolved organic entities.

As a group, Pisceans are fond of artichokes, which is quite mysterious since it is almost impossible to discover any other consensus among these people regarding their food preferences (with the possible exception of alcoholic beverages). Pisceans are the poet-mystics of the zodiac and their private feelings, moods and dreams are their lives' greatest realities. To a Pisces, empirical observation is only one limited conceptual approach to life.

Given this, there is a particularity to the individual taste of any Pisces that can be quite unnerving. They won't or can't explain their deep likes and dislikes, which appear embedded in Pisceans' psychological history. Collectively, they are extremely sensitive to most stimuli, but it's impossible to predict how any one of them will react in a given situation.

Fine. So what do you fix them for dinner?

To start on the negative side, it is well worth directly asking what they *don't* like. Some Pisceans *hate* entire menu categories, all soups or all frozen desserts for example. Dining out they can have radical aversions to most anything—buffet home-cooking restaurants, celebrity chefs, any departure from vanilla plain.

Conversely, soup may be their absolute favorite food. They may adore the least worthy of over-publicized gourmet restaurants. Burnt caramel ripple gelato may be a passion.

A Pisces' tastes, to reiterate, are largely the product of private psychological associations. Whatever you serve or wherever you host, the prevailing spirit is all-important. Pisceans will absolutely recoil from anything served in a hostile, strife-filled or dirty environment, and will be immediately attracted to anything that gently caters to their own natural sense of solicitude.

It is worth keeping this solicitude in mind when Pisceans offer to do the cooking. Most Pisceans genuinely like to cook, and many are quite expert in handling subtle flavor combinations and in making aesthetically pleasing plate presentations, but they have a strong fear of failing to please and will frequently apologize over their best efforts. Constant *sincere* assurance that you love what has been served will never be too much of a good thing for Pisces.

This may all tend to make the Pisces seem a little too sensitive and a little too remote from common-sense reaction. Probably one should err a little in this direction when confronting a Pisces. But remember the artichoke.

A lot of people merely admire and eat the leaves, believing they have thereby extracted the artichoke experience. But a Pisces never overlooks the deep experience of a hidden heart. Never.

How preoccupied are you with the subjects of food and dining?

I hate when people tell me I'm fat and that I have psychological problems. I love my mother. There are no secret reasons. I just feel like eating.

What's your favorite cookbook?

James Beard's *American Cooking.* I think it is. I'm not sure.

Ten Foods a Pisces Needs to Survive on a Deserted Island

Noodles • Melted cheese • Eggs • Beef • Chicken
Milk • Broccoli • Oranges • Artichokes • Alcoholic beverages

What ten foods would you need to survive on a deserted island?

I hate this part. Can we skip it? Can we do it last?

Pisces Island

On Pisces Island you can get everywhere by walking. The scale is small and everyone knows everyone else. This way, Pisces eliminates two key sources of personal anxiety, automobiles and strangers.

To understand Pisceans is to appreciate their fear and reverence regarding the unknown. To Pisceans, the most unpleasant realities all start out as nothings and nobodies coming out of nowhere. When your spirit is attuned to this process, you're not real eager to seek out challenging situations or surroundings.

So it is the lack of anything suggesting aggression that is Pisces Island's most arresting feature. Stores, schools, parks and houses are reminiscent of the little villages bordering the tracks of children's train sets. The place is for each inhabitant their "own little world."

Where all is familiar, the Pisces is quite gregarious. They like the emotions of group interaction. In any situation, Pisces is a bellwether to the mood of the crowd.

Restaurants on Pisces Island are pleasant, clean and comfortable, featuring a cuisine based on familiar foods thoroughly cooked (no bacteria-laden steak tartares for this group) yet sensitively seasoned. Markets are attractive and amply stocked without being conceptually burdensome. In all shopping situations there are well-mannered and competent service personnel to help guide poor Pisces through the jungles of selection.

However quaint and tame all this sounds, Pisces is not a stranger to broad vistas, although these are usually of the interior landscape. One catches a glimpse of the hidden Pisces perception by observing the Pisceans' homes, most built with verandas facing exquisitely lovely and endless tracts of water and sky. Pisces' private heaven is to sit out on one of these porches, to sip a glass of wine and to dissolve back into the unreality which precedes, coexists with and outlasts all reality.

The island has a lot of liquor stores.

Do you prefer eating out or eating at home?

It depends on who's doing the cooking. If it's me, I'd just as soon eat at home.

Pisces Favorites (an impossible task)

Vegetable: artichokes (broccoli, carrots, etc.)
Fruit: oranges (peaches, berries, etc.)
Starch: pasta (potatoes, rice, etc.)
Source of protein: beef (poultry, seafood, etc.)
Bread product: crusty sourdough (crusty French, crusty Italian, etc.)
Dairy product: cheese (milk, ice cream, etc.)
Spice or herb: garlic (cilantro, thyme, etc.)
Condiment: mustard (horseradish, maple syrup, etc.)
Ice cream flavor: Neapolitan (etc.)
Pizza topping: mushrooms (sausage, artichoke hearts, etc.)
Candy: boxed chocolates (nut centers, caramel centers, etc.)
Cookie: oatmeal raisin (pecan sandies, mint Oreos, etc.)
Sandwich: cheeseburger (bacon-lettuce-tomato, corned beef, etc.)
Soup: old-fashioned chicken soup (French onion, cream of broccoli, etc.)
Soft drink: Cola!
Beer: full-flavored
Wine: full-bodied
Liquor: whiskey
Liqueur: Cognac or Irish Cream
Comfort food: a very personal matter
Celebration food: pie à la mode
Junk food: French fries
Sexy food: scampi

What is your favorite fruit?

> Pineapple, kiwi and watermelon are the only three fruits I'll put in my mouth.

What is your favorite liqueur?

> Anything put in front of me.

Pisces Diet and Health

The Pisces has this thing about germs and illness. As if every bacterium of the universe is secretly plotting against them. These enemies lurk everywhere, particularly on wet towels and in strange foods.

This radical indisposition towards contaminants can take on crusade-like proportions for Pisces (witness the career of Adelle Davis). At first it may just seem they're being practical, and then you notice that they're washing utensils coming from the clean silverware drawer. During exceptional periods, actual illness or pregnancy for example, this behavior can become so intense that a Pisces will refuse to move from pre-sanitized zones or depart one crumb from a rigidly orchestrated "safe" diet.

Clearly, though, Pisceans are not amiss in recognizing that any act of ingestion has an impact upon the consuming organism. Pisceans are both smart and sensitive enough to realize that they are particularly prone to powerful reactions from radical alterations in their diet. The most tranquil Pisceans usually have the simplest diets and are smart enough to do without too much alcohol.

Ultimately, the successful Pisces approach to diet tends to be a matter of avoiding unknowns and cherishing favorites. If they have a prevailing dietary theory it is that you should eat what you really feel like eating and avoid what you don't. On the rare occasions that Pisceans go on formal diets they invariably gain weight as food becomes inordinately implanted in the forefront of consciousness.

Adelle Davis aside, they're not generally inclined to publicly debate dietary beliefs. But Pisceans never play it fast and loose when it comes to convictions. Beliefs, even about proteins and carbohydrates, are not frivolous matters to them.

Do you ever diet?

Not really. If I diet I get too conscious of food.

Do you have any nutritional habits or beliefs?

Whatever your body craves you should eat because you need it.

Ten More Foods Most Pisces Like a Whole Lot

Ocean fish • Carrots • Lettuce • Rice • Chocolate • French fries
Cake • Salty snacks • Jams and jellies • More alcoholic beverages

Things You Should Not Feed a Pisces

Anything obviously experimental in flavor or appearance
Food that falls on the floor

What are some foods or flavors that turn you off?

I can't stand liver. When I was a kid my parents tried to pass it off as steak. But I fixed them. I threw up.

Pisces Homefood

Pisceans are extremely sentimental and usually bond closely with their homes and possessions. Much like Cancer, they are prone to surrounding themselves with a lifetime's worth of personal memorabilia. Even if cluttered, however, their homes are always snug and peaceful because home is where a Pisces needs to feel uncompromisingly secure.

Many of Pisces' tastes are formed in childhood and there is most always a great appreciation of some aspect of home cooking. A good tuna noodle casserole, a homemade layer cake, the Thanksgiving turkey—these can be powerfully nostalgic to Pisces. Whatever their age, Pisceans enjoy mealtimes as protective gatherings of the clan.

When it comes to their own menu making they almost always select familiar foods. Pisces cooks have a real talent for enhancing common fare through artful selection of spices and condiments. Their cupboards and refrigerators are usually stocked with multiple brands of mustards, jams, laurel leaves, etc. Pisceans always enjoy comparing the subtle differences between similar favorite products.

Probably their very favorite things to cook are stews and casseroles. They like the free-flowing creativity of such dishes and, while they are fearful of secret ingredients in dishes served to them, love to be the perpetrators of savory surprises themselves. Their major culinary quirk is hating to clean up, because cooking should be an art rather than a chore, and when you're cleaning up it means everyone's about to go separate ways.

After everyone leaves, Pisceans feel sad for a while, but they eventually come to realize how much they need and enjoy being left alone. Just about then a little liqueur, a few chocolates, some quiet music and a comfortable chair start to sound real good. In a Pisces home they're around somewhere.

Do you like to cook?

Yes. It's therapy. Nobody tells me what to do but me.

No. Nothing comes out the way it should.

What do you like to cook?

I like salads, except for the salad I made tonight.

What's the most interesting thing in your refrigerator?

Four bunches of green onions bought on four separate occasions. I never eat green onions.

Pisces Breakfast

Most Pisceans do not like breakfast. Okay, I'm sure you know the one Pisces who loves breakfast. I told you this wasn't going to be easy.

It's just that most Pisceans aren't the sort of people to charge right into the busy day. Dreaminess is their natural state. In the early morning, arising from the heaviest sleep period, it's pretty hard for a Pisces to make a concerted effort towards something as mundane as preparing breakfast.

If they do make it into the kitchen they can, with some effort, manage coffee and toast. If they're actually hungry they will be quite pleased to discover dinner leftovers, although these will be consumed only if nobody else is around. In fact, if nobody is there to criticize, Pisces is fully capable of preparing a bacon, lettuce and tomato sandwich, fries and perhaps a chocolate malt.

When dining with company, Pisceans' breakfast choices will be a good deal more conservative. They usually go for the classic cereals like Cheerios, or for cinnamon rolls or simple bacon and egg plates. If they're letting their hair down they may risk pancakes with real maple syrup.

While they generally do prefer to be alone in the morning, Pisceans have many romantic fantasies that are garnished with the rising sun. But these fantasies only marginally involve breakfast foods. Very marginally.

What do you like to eat for breakfast?

My favorite breakfast is a Southern breakfast—a roll in bed with honey.

What do you like to have if you're going to enjoy a special breakfast?

Lunch.

Who is your favorite companion for breakfast?

I want to be alone! I'm fierce in the morning.

Pisces Breakfast Favorites

Juices: grapefruit, orange
Fruits: canteloupe, papaya
Cereals: Cheerios, Grape Nuts, Rice Krispies
Sweet rolls: sticky buns
Breads: anything toasted
Egg dish: scrambled with bacon
Other: plain pancakes with real maple syrup and sausages

Pisces Awayfood

Just because Pisceans are generally sensitive and a little withdrawn is no reason to underestimate their taste. Pisceans frequently lead lives touched by music, theater, fine arts and other complex emotive endeavors for which their sensitivity particularly well suits them. They are no lightweights when it comes to appreciating depth of intention.

Pisceans know good cooking. When dining out, their very favorite places are the ones that serve "the best food anywhere." They patronize establishments that feature wholesome first-quality ingredients that are cooked and served with artful, not outrageous or otherwise distracting, enhancements.

This does not mean Pisceans are snobs about dining out. They can be happy in a good delicatessen or even a fast food restaurant. But they expect to see some intelligent concern with quality and imagination on the menu.

Pisceans also expect to see a lot of cleanliness and an acceptable level of service. Pisceans can get ill just looking at a dirty rest room. And they can become heartsick if service is other than helpful, courteous and kind. Interestingly, Pisceans are usually pretty big fans of McDonald's and other well-known chains, especially on unknown turf, simply because they can count on the cleanliness and service factors.

Sometimes Pisceans seem followers of fashion and their favorite restaurant choices a little hackneyed, but a Pisces simply appreciates a restaurant that is capable of earning a broad public reputation. This is at least an indication of a certain level of "safeness" to the dining experience, with the potential for something more. The Pisces generally trusts qualified critical authority, and is usually more impressed to read about a place in the paper than to hear of it from friends.

And for all of this, it sometimes seems that the only factor that really matters to Pisces is a restaurant's atmosphere. Particularly on vacations, which Pisceans deeply cherish and require, they love sitting in absolutely gorgeous environments and totally blissing out. Most of the time, though, they just feel more comfortable at home.

What's your favorite new restaurant trend?

I don't go to a lot of trendy restaurants. I don't like the unexpected. I go to the same places over and over.

Are there any new trends in the restaurant scene you don't like?

I'm not crazy about sushi bars.

Romantic Menus for Pisces

To romance him:

Table: French bread and sweet butter
Appetizer: baked oysters
Soup: cream of artichoke
Entrée: sliced steak au poivre; julienne celery and carrots
Wine: French red Burgundy
Dessert: Grand Marnier soufflé; Cognac and coffee

To romance her:

Table: linen and candlelight
Appetizer: steamed artichoke with drawn butter
Salad: green with fresh herb dressing
Entrée: sautéed veal scallops with wild mushrooms; risotto with cheese
Wine: French Chardonnay
Dessert: green apple tart; coffee and liqueur

Pisces Food Fantasy

To Pisceans, the things that really matter are the things that really matter. They may have sexual fantasies and food fantasies and all the other sorts of fantasies one can have, but what they really have is an abiding love for the people they love. More than mere fantasy, when Pisceans have peak contact with those they love, this is for Pisceans a state of grace.

"Peaks" can sometimes be taken in a literal sense, as the following description of a "perfect meal" by a young Pisces waitress indicates. Her words will touch the souls of all her astrological brethren.

The perfect meal took place last summer in the mountains of Switzerland. My two brothers, my mother, my father and I invaded a small shop and filled a grocery basket with assorted cheeses, pâtés, spreads and a German white wine. We found a secluded mountain stream to chill the wine and ate our feast with Swiss army knives.

Pisceans dream in vivid detail. And they don't even have to be asleep.

What would be your idea of the perfect meal?

There isn't anything I never had that I would want to try.

Mom's Graham Cracker Cake

submitted by Carol Haddix

Cake:
1 cup flour
1 cup sugar
3 1/2 t. baking powder
3/4 t. salt
2 cups graham cracker crumbs
　(not packaged crumbs)
1 cup plus 2 T. milk
3/4 cup vegetable shortening
1 1/2 t. vanilla
3 eggs

Filling:
1 1/2 cups milk
1 vanilla bean or 1 1/2 t. vanilla
　extract
1/2 cup sugar
1/4 cup flour
4 egg yolks, beaten

Preheat oven to 375°. Into mixer bowl sift flour, sugar, baking powder, and salt. Add graham cracker crumbs, shortening, milk and vanilla. Beat at low speed until crumbs are moistened, then beat 2 minutes at medium speed. Add eggs, beating well after each addition. Pour batter into two 9" greased and paper-lined cake pans. Bake 25-30 minutes or until top springs back when pressed lightly with fingertip. Remove from oven and cool 10 minutes. Remove from pan and cool on cake racks. Slice each layer in half horizontally.

For filling, scald milk in saucepan with vanilla bean or vanilla extract. In top of double boiler over boiling water mix sugar, flour, and egg yolks. Beat until light. Remove vanilla bean from milk and add milk gradually to creamed mixture. Stir until well blended. Cook, stirring, until just before mixture reaches boiling point and thickens. Remove from heat and continue stirring to cool. Cool completely. Spread over cake layers and stack. Frost cake with sweetened whipped cream or buttercream frosting. Makes one 9" layer cake.

Chocolate Silk

submitted by Peggy Jo Gustin

1 6-oz. package semisweet chocolate pieces
1/2 cup boiling water
1/2 cup peanut butter, smooth or chunky-style
3 T. sugar
4 eggs

Place chocolate pieces in blender container. Blend at medium speed 10 seconds. Scrape down sides of blender container with rubber spatula, if necessary. Add boiling water. Blend at medium speed 5 seconds. Add peanut butter, sugar and eggs. Blend at medium speed until smooth, about 30 to 45 seconds. Pour into 6 individual serving cups, dishes or prebaked tart shells. Refrigerate until firm or overnight. Garnish with whipped cream or nuts, if desired.

Intoxicating Chocolate Cake

submitted by Nancy Kelly

1 box chocolate fudge cake mix
1 box instant chocolate fudge
   pudding mix
4 eggs
1/2 cup salad oil
1 cup port wine

Glaze:
1/4 lb. butter
1 cup sugar
1/3 cup port wine

Mix cake ingredients for 3 minutes. Pour batter into a well buttered bundt pan and bake in a 325° oven for one hour. To make glaze, boil butter and sugar for 1 minute. Remove from heat and stir in port wine. Remove cake from oven and immediately pour glaze over it. Allow to set for 2 minutes. Remove from pan and cool. When cake is at room temperature, sprinkle with confectioners' sugar.

Guasacaca

submitted by Barbara Lang

(It sounds like something a baby produces but really is very good!)

1 pork tenderloin, 2-3 lbs
salt
freshly ground black pepper

Preheat oven to 400°. Dry the pork tenderloin with a paper towel and then sprinkle with salt and pepper. Set pork on an oiled roasting pan and bake for 10 minutes. Reduce heat to 325°. Roast the tenderloin for 25 minutes per pound. Meat temperature should be 155°-165°. Remove from oven and let the tenderloin rest for 10 minutes. This allows the meat to reabsorb some its juices and finish cooking. The internal temperature of the pork will rise to about 165°-170°. Carve tenderloin and serve with Avocado Salsa Verde (recipe follows). Serves six to eight. Serve with Inglenook Vineyards Estate Bottled 1983 Sauvignon Blanc.

Avocado Salsa Verde

submitted by Barbara Lang

2 T. white wine vinegar
2 T. fresh lime juice
3/4 cup olive oil
1/2 T. pickled serrano chiles, finely diced
1/2 T. cilantro, finely chopped

2 T. parsley, finely chopped
1 garlic clove, mashed
2 T. onion, finely diced
5 ripe avocados, cut into 1/4" pieces
salt and pepper to taste

Combine the vinegar and lime juice in a small glass or stainless steel bowl. Slowly whisk in oil. Set dressing aside. In a large bowl, add the remaining ingredients. Pour the dressing over the salsa and gently mix. Taste the seasonings. Even though the salsa may not initially taste hot, be aware that the pickled serrano chiles will develop in flavor. Salsa can be made a day in advance.

California Citrus Chicken

submitted by Marilyn Hawkes, who got it from her brother Marvin, also a Pisces, but one who is outraged by the subject of astrology and will probably be p—d off that this is why Marilyn wanted the recipe.

5 boneless chicken breasts

Coating
1/2 t. salt
1/2 t. paprika
1/2 t. white pepper
1/2 t. basil
1/2 t. rosemary

Citrus Mix
2 t. orange juice
2 t. fresh lime juice
2 t. fresh lemon juice
1/4 cup white wine

3 T. strawberry banana yogurt

Mix coating ingredients in a small bowl. Place chicken and mixture into a brown paper bag and shake until mixture coats the chicken. Heat a very small amount of oil in a skillet and brown chicken on both sides. Add citrus mix and poach for 15-20 minutes. Remove chicken to warm oven. To the pan juices add yogurt. Mix well and reduce for 5 minutes. Pour over chicken. Enjoy!

Chicken Divan

submitted by Toddy Chase

2 10-oz. packages frozen broccoli
4 T. butter
4 T. flour
2 cups chicken stock
1/2 cup heavy cream, whipped

3 T. sherry
salt and pepper
1 cup grated parmesan cheese
16 generous portions chicken,
  preferably breasts

Preheat oven to 375°. Cook broccoli according to package directions. Place in a large casserole. Melt butter in a saucepan, blend in flour. Add chicken stock and cook and stir until smooth. Cook for 10 minutes. Add cream, sherry and seasonings. Pour half the sauce over the broccoli; to the remaining sauce add the grated cheese. Arrange chicken pieces on broccoli in the casserole; pour remaining sauce over the chicken. Sprinkle with additional cheese. Bake uncovered for 30 minutes.

Lamb Shanks

submitted by Jo Manzi

Wash 3 lamb shanks. Put in a pan with sliced raw potatoes, minced garlic, basil, grated cheese, salt and pepper, a little oil, a few chopped tomatoes and 1 glass of water. Bake uncovered at 350° for 1 hour.

Some Pisces Food Personalities

Richard Melman, founder and president, Lettuce Entertain You, Chicago, Illinois

Warner LeRoy, owner, Tavern on the Green, Maxwell's Plum, New York City

Bill Wilkinson, president, Campton Place, San Francisco, California

Carol Haddix, food guide editor, *Chicago Tribune*

Recipe Index

Miscellaneous

Desserts